Best wishes

Charles J. mark

Tell It As It Is

by
Charles Parker

A NO HOLDS BARRED
Story Of A Family Living
With Severe Autism

authorHOUSE®

AuthorHouse™ UK Ltd.
500 Avebury Boulevard
Central Milton Keynes, MK9 2BE
www.authorhouse.co.uk
Phone: 08001974150

First published by AuthorHouse 9/7/2007

ISBN: 978-1-4343-2861-8 (sc)

Printed in the United States of America
Bloomington, Indiana

This book is printed on acid-free paper.

Table of Contents

It's Well Worth A Read!

This is not an academic text- book, but a from-the heart account of one family, living with and caring for a severely autistic child.

It MAY move you to tears, and it will certainly give you a clearer insight into the trials, tribulations and amazingly sometimes JOY of being a parent in this family.

Phyllis Painter- Retired Teacher

and one of the Proof Readers of this book

Dedication

This book is dedicated to my son Christopher and my wonderfully supportive family

Acknowledgements

I have thoroughly enjoyed writing this book, it has certainly kept me out of mischief, many nights until two or three in the morning but I could not have achieved the finished product without the help and encouragement of my dear wife Tina.

I would also like to thank the members of the Hampshire Autistic Society for their contribution particularly in the promotion.

To those people who took the time and trouble to help make chapter twenty-five, What the people think, so interesting, please accept my gratitude.

My thanks go also to the ladies who have spent many hours of their time proofreading my work.

No book can successfully reach the shelves of a bookstore without the support and professional input of a good publisher and as this is my very first works I would like to thank Ross Thompson wholeheartedly for his advice and support.

To anyone I may have missed, that have made a contribution to the successful completion and promotion of this book, thank you.

Finally I want to make a special mention of my son Charles for his contribution, thank you son.

Preface

"I think your child may be autistic"

Those words are probably the most devastating that many parents have ever heard. Hearing those words could easily destroy some families. Those words could easily have destroyed us as a family but as you read on you will find out differently. Our philosophy is that life is all about choices, whether you choose to give up or fight on is your decision, but hopefully our words will be of some encouragement to help all of those in doubt to take the positive approach and fight on.

We want you to take a step into our lives. If you don't know already what it is like, find out how an autistic child can completely change your life. We are not hiding anything; it is the bare, undiluted truth. The heartaches, the fears and the joy that we have learnt to accept.

Where have we gone for help? How have we achieved so many goals? Perhaps more importantly, how have we remained sane? So many of our customers and friends say you've always got a smile on your face, how do you do it? Well if you don't smile you would probably cry.

Hopefully we have whetted your appetite and you want to find out more, but just before you turn the page here's our little secret.

You see, just like many of you we have a mirror in our bedroom. Unlike most we use it every morning. You see when we get up we look in that mirror and smile and you know what.

EVERY DAY WITHOUT FAIL WE GET A SMILE BACK!
Charles and Tina Parker

Chapter 1
Happy As A Pig in Muck

"Happy as a PIG IN MUCK"! That's exactly how we both felt, both having problems in the past but now really happy. Here we were just over two years into our marriage and we had two beautiful boys, Charlie and Christopher. Add those to two older children, Anna and Brian, from a previous marriage and what more could one want?

Many people found it odd when we married, with so many years between us but we were not worried one little bit. We were happy, in love and with a fantastic family. We were so lucky, the older children taking to the Charlie and Christopher so well.

Anna wanted to be a little mum and do everything she could and even Brian volunteered to change nappies. Well for a while anyway until the novelty wore off.

Essentially we had everything now, a great family, good jobs, adequate home and ambition to do well.

So why have I started this book by telling you about the past? It is so important that a comparison can be made between what seemed like "HEAVEN" to what was soon to confront us, when we heard those words;

"I think your child might be autistic!"

To this day Tina and I still find that short but so significant sentence ringing in our ears. Did we really understand at that point what it meant? "No, of course not" but we did know it was certainly not good news. We had both heard of autism but like so many of the population did not truly understand the implications.

One thing is for sure that we understood that it was serious, both of us turning to tears after returning home from that consultation. Each trying to console the other with thoughts that they, the doctors, might just have got it wrong. Living in the hope that another thought that Chris was in fact deaf and not autistic, yes we were sure this could be the case. It could also be a case of Glue ear; yes that'll be it. That is until several hearing tests finally ruled out any problems with Christopher's hearing. Were we soon to find out the worst?

During all of this uncertainty we kept ourselves going by believing that looking at Chris, with this autism thing, wouldn't really be so bad. We could cope, he's not that much different to any other child. Family and friends tried in their own way to reassure us that all would be well, not knowing or understanding what autism was all about.

The paediatrician was organising a formal diagnosis which would take two visits a week and last for up to ten weeks, but both of us being anxious started surfing the net in search of answers, looking for clues, looking for hope probably that the professionals were wrong. We also started to look for reasons why. If our son was autistic what had suddenly caused the change in him. He had been given his jabs at about thirteen months and it was shortly after this that we started to notice certain changes in his behaviour. Was it something he had contracted through one of us, a faulty gene?

Now this is where we had to be responsible and sensible parents. Did it really matter what caused it? Would knowing suddenly turn the clock back? To Hell! If the proposed diagnosis proved our little boy was indeed autistic we had to just get on with it. We had to be strong, we had to stay together. We had to support each other and be there, an ever-present shoulder to cry on. Very often this has proved to be a case of crying on one and another's shoulders, but that togetherness is why we are together today, still striving to achieve everything that will improve both ours and our children's lives.

Chapter 2
Leading to the gates of Hell

Wordsworth House in Southampton was the place where Christopher's diagnosis would take place and boy, were we nervous that first morning? Knowing very little and certainly not knowing anyone other than the clinical psychologist, who had visited us at home to check Chris fitted the required criteria, we gingerly made our way inside.

To our amazement we found it and everyone associated with Wordsworth to be so friendly, just when you need to see a smile, feel a warm welcome and to be put at ease. Our first impression was that of a play school, there being other children already being diagnosed and various adults working on a one to one basis. It was explained that rather than just wait around, it was hoped that we would join other parents, all in the same position as us, in a discussion group, and we jumped at this opportunity. It was actually amazing that some of the mums and dads chose to join the group but never got actively involved. We were the gasbags, for want of a better description, taking every opportunity to question whomever it was leading the discussion or to try to learn something from parents further down the line than us. Why waste a chance like this to find out what might lie ahead?

Each week Chris would meet and work with the Psychologist, Speech and language therapist and a specialized play nurse. It didn't take long for them to realise that when he chose to do his own thing, they had a real job on their hands to stop him. He was also clever enough to fool these guys when he wanted to by just shutting down. After a few weeks he seemed to almost look forward to going and wanted to drag us in before we had even locked the car. For us we would live in hope over those ten long weeks that someone had made a mistake, maybe Chris was just a late developer but deep down we knew we had to be prepared for the worst. This little bundle of joy of ours that started life just like most other children, playing appropriately, giving us hugs, kisses and plenty of eye contact was basically lost, probably gone for ever. He had started developing repetitive habits, none more dangerous than wrapping anything he could find that resembled string around his fingers and, on more than one occasion, cutting off the blood supply to his fingertips.

The big day arrived. The professionals had reached their verdict and we were invited in to meet them. Although everyone was friendly it felt rather like we were in front of a Kangaroo Court, with only one outcome; Guilty As Charged.

Mind it didn't seem so bad after all. The psychologist, chairing the meeting, confirmed what had been suspected that Chris had autism and developmental delay Now we had done our homework on this subject and knew that there were varying types of autism, some mild some severe. "So where is he on the autistic spectrum"? we piped up and anxiously waited for the reply.

Now here's why it didn't seem so bad because we were told that the team believed Christopher's autism was on the severe end of the spectrum. Well, we thought as we went home, if that's severe and it's not going to get any worse than this we could cope with that, no trouble.

Little did we know. You see, whilst we had been reading up on the subject we either hadn't read enough or we were so emotionally affected we had not taken it in. What we did know was that he was still our son, our darling little blond beauty and no matter what was wrong with him we would love him just the same.

Chapter 3
Sentenced To Life

On at least two occasions that we can recall a couple of our customers have come out with the same statement, that we have basically been given a life sentence. We hadn't really thought about it that way until the first person mentioned it, but sure as eggs are eggs, they were not far wrong.

When we arrived home the day judgement was made we were stunned. Stunned; so emotionally affected that we didn't know which way to go next. What would the future hold? What would happen when Chris was old enough for school? What would other people think? On this thought it was not long before we found out. Many of our family and friends were very sympathetic but at the same time really did not truly understand the problem. Things like "He'll be alright", "He'll grow out of it", and we had those and lots more all said in an attempt to make us feel better.

The real hurt came however as birthdays and other parties came and went. Parties that our sons had normally been invited to but were now ostracized. How could anyone do this to our boys? Was Chris that different? Did he suddenly grow an extra head? All right. He had started screeching and was more difficult to control, but was this enough to exclude both him and his brother? To this day that problem is still there, with very few invitations arriving on the doormat for our little chaps.

We are pretty sure that the psychologist who conducted the diagnosis procedure had already read into our minds and knew that we were prepared to do whatever was needed to ensure that Christopher always had the best from life. She had mentioned to us that Southampton University, in conjunction with Southampton City Council, were to conduct a survey or clinical assessment to prove to the government that ABA, Approved behavioural analysis, would be beneficial to autistic children. Having spoken to the psychologist we realised that this was something we were going to have for our son. Notice, "We were going to have for our son". There was no question of hoping that we would get him on the course. The course in question was called SCAMP.

We put his name forward, and then kept hot on the tail of everyone involved in the selection process. At this point the educational psychologist got involved and the supervisor from the university that would run the course, both of whom visited us at home and agreed that Christopher fitted the criteria they were looking for. This would mean that at almost exactly three years old he would be the first to commence the course. Mind this could not begin until a number of tutors had been found and trained. It also meant that as parents we had to commit ourselves to doing some of the work and so agreed to attend the training course at Southampton University with the tutors.

Now lets just try to tell you, in our words, how this ABA system worked. We first of all had to dedicate a room of the house, in our case the sun lounge, to become Christopher's classroom for the next two years. The course was extremely intensive and involved two three hour sessions each day for seven days a week and that even included many of the bank holidays.

It is important to say that by this time Chris had all but given up on speech, save plenty of screeching and eye contact was also at a premium. These were to be two of the major issues to be worked on initially.

For want of better words the best way to describe the ABA method would be to liken it to training a dog. You do this and we will give you a treat. For a very long time it appeared to work and Chris showed progress in many areas but he was not as stupid as some would make out. He soon realised that once he had done something once there was no need to demonstrate this skill again. The pressure on him was constant from the tutors, not their fault for sure, as the powers above were likewise putting pressure on them to show results. On more than one occasion Chris would simply switch off, lay down his head on the table and go sound asleep. This was the end for the day. Just think about it, six hours a day is one more hour than any child does at a normal school and in hindsight too much for a child of Christopher's age but for then we had to stick with it.

You remember we mentioned that we too had to get involved in the work. Well this was where we became unstuck. Being a mum or dad and then suddenly trying to wear a different hat just did not work, at least not for us. We found it so very difficult to be so consistently firm on our little angel and at the same time try to find time to keep our businesses running. As time went by more and more was expected of Christopher and it has to be said that in many ways we did see improvement, particularly with his speech returning, albeit mostly echolalia. Problems arose as Chris neared school age, one being the fight to get him into the school we felt was best for him, whilst others were content to place him into a school for children with moderate and varied disabilities. We eventually won that battle and he started at the school of our choice two days a week in the summer term of 2003.

Probably the biggest problem related to the Scamp project was that more and more we felt that there was a take over bid as to who would dictate Christopher's future. Intensity grew not only for our son but also for us as parents. Christopher was being pushed harder and harder, we were told that we should be accompanied to all hospital and doctor appointments and the teachers at the school where Chris had started nursery felt their hands were tied. You see whilst he had started school he was still on the Scamp project and a tutor would go into school with him. The school had its methods of teaching and at that time were confident they could help Christopher to progress. With the conflict of opinions between teachers, tutors and us it became obvious we had to show that as parents we had the last word and Christopher was withdrawn from Scamp with about twenty months completed. Probably something that helped us make our minds up was when the head teacher at his school said it was important for Christopher to have time where he was allowed to be autistic.

Please do not think we are ungrateful or in any way dissatisfied with the help Christopher received but sometimes one must question whether all of this was really to benefit your child or to fulfil someone else's ambitions.

We were the ones at the coal face, looking after Chris twenty four seven, making sure he was always safe, listening to his incessant screaming day and night, spending night after night without sleep and wondering what his next habit would bring in the way of surprise.

Chapter 4
Habits Of A Lifetime

From the early days right up to the present Christopher has had some really disgusting habits and some that are nothing short of dangerous. Let us for now share with you just a few that took place from the very start up until he went to school. What is important to remember is that any one of these could come back into play at any time; it's like a never-ending circle of events, not a wheel of fortune but a wheel of mystery and intrigue?

The first that we can recall was quite a dangerous habit whereby he would look for anything that resembled string and wrap it around his arms or more often his fingers. Very often you would put on your shoes and wonder why they slipped on so easily, then realise Chris had borrowed your laces. If he wasn't wrapping the string around his fingers then he was spinning it around and around. Actually a very funny thing happened when we went to hospital for blood tests around this period. The play nurse, a really kind man called Rob, asked how he could help distract Chris and when told Chris liked string he went off to fetch some. Unfortunately he could not find any handy but not to be beaten promptly took the laces out of his shoes. Chris didn't care where it came from but the blood was taken without too much fuss.

Biting was, and still is, a constant worry, biting anyone in range or himself if he needs to take out his frustrations. In the past he has bitten his fingers raw, causing them to bleed and obviously become very sore. It is so strange though that he does not seem to show any signs that he is in pain. There are a couple of times that come to mind when his biting someone else really was a concern. Firstly when we were in Tescos one night doing the shopping and had both him and his brother Charlie sat next to one another in the trolley. Suddenly there was this deafening cry, no a high pitched scream, which happened to be Charlie as Chris had laid into his finger and under no circumstances was he going to let go. What a game we had securing Charlie's release and what an audience we had as well. Most people will have no doubt wondered why we had allowed it to happen, and probably concluded that we were bad parents.

His next major biting experience was directed towards his dad. Yes, whilst driving the car, there was occasion to try to stop Chris from once again biting his brother but when my hand went back over the shoulder he took hold of my index finger and just like a bull terrier would not leave go. Somehow we pulled in on the side of the road and for a brief moment he released his grip. The finger he bit was numb and the feeling did not return completely for some two weeks. The strange thing is of course if you make a big issue of anything he does he will see it as a reinforcement and want to do it again. On quite a number of times we had to bandage Charlie's wounds including bites to his back after Chris had forced his older brother to the floor.

Along with the biting came one which never failed to get us noticed and still to this day can draw the attention of plenty nosey, ignorant people. Just imagine yourself out with your family. Maybe you're at the cinema, perhaps a church service or a family get together. Everyone is fairly quiet, engrossed or focussed on what's going on. Then suddenly out of nowhere your child screams at the top of their voice. Not just once but repeatedly, over and over again, getting louder and louder. People look around at you and you just know under their breath they are saying, "shut that child up!"

Just how do you feel? Hoping the ground will open up, wishing you were an ostrich so you could bury your head in the sand.

Perhaps you start to get the picture now of how it is for us nearly every time we attempt to go somewhere as a family. We used to feel just like that ostrich only instead of burying our head in the sand we would quickly collect our things together and make a hasty retreat. We have been to Weddings, birthday parties, the cinema and even out to do a bit of shopping when we have just had to give in and go home. We did not want to ruin things for other people. Times change though and you do become tougher. Although there are places such as the cinema where we dare not take Chris we do try now and then to take him to a park or visit the odd relative. The difference being we have become thick skinned and really don't care what the "normal" people think. We have as much right to take our children out and about as the next man.

Another extremely bad habit, that takes little reinforcement to achieve an encore is spitting. Christopher has never been fussy. If he feels like spitting he will and this is one that really gets the natives going. Even with years of seeing him perform it is something that we find hard to accept, mainly I suppose because it is an antisocial behaviour. He has actually progressed from just spitting on the floor or on you if you're close enough. He has now worked out that if he spits in his hand he can actually project his weapon somewhat further, throwing it at the walls or windows and then taking great pleasure in standing there admiring his work. To take this one step further he has learnt that better distances can be achieved if he sucks a piece of paper or sometimes a part of his nappy and then launches it on its way. We are not proud to have a child with such a strong throwing arm, or one that uses such disgusting weapons but all one can do is try to distract him, move him on to something different. You tell him NO and he loves it.

Pouring, he loves that as well! Every visitor that dare enter our home is warned, "Do not take your eye off of your cup!" Christopher needs little time and certainly no encouragement to tip out anything he finds lying around. It may be your drink he spots but quite often it is something that causes much more inconvenience and frustration. Just think about how busy you are when it comes to dishing up the Sunday dinner, trying to do several things all at once, making sure the dinner arrives on the table hot. Bear in mind too that you are always engaged in cooking something completely different for Christopher, until recently it was his chicken nuggets or perhaps chicken nuggets or just for a change more chicken nuggets. Thank God we have moved on a little.

Where were we? The pouring. Now just imagine you're in the middle of dishing up and the phone rings, there's a knock at the front door or simply Mother Nature calls. You only have to be off duty for one brief moment for Chris to mount his attack. Just a few weeks back he reminded us of one of his perhaps worst culinary ideas. Having demonstrated this very recipe before I suppose we should know better, but there is nothing he loves more than to grab the gravy jug and pour the whole lot into the custard, made ready for pudding.

How annoying is that? The dinner gets cold whilst you wash up the jugs and remake more of the same and what's even more frustrating is that when Chris chooses to perform this particular act it just happens to be when you have no more gravy powder or custard powder in the cupboard.

It would be better to say this particular habit is not just pouring but tipping as well. Many is the time when out in the garden he decides that flowers do not belong in pots so out they come, followed very often by the pot being thrown and therefore broken as a result.

Tearing is another habit that causes us so much despair. Ripping up any papers he can lay his hands on, whether it be post that has arrived, books that Charlie may have left around and of course the decorative borders around some of the rooms. Without doubt, more frustrating and certainly more expensive is his persistent tearing of his clothes. We have spent hundreds of pounds replacing his clothes, bedclothes and indeed the specialised sleep suits, which were bought in an attempt to keep him out of his nappy. Go into his bedroom in the morning and one might be met with Chris making sure you are aware of what he has done by saying "Oh Poor Blanky!" Poor blanky indeed, it is often reduced to strips no wider than an inch or two wide. "Poor Pillow" as he smiles at the mound of stuffing in the corner.

Now "Posting," that is the one habit that nearly got us into deep trouble with the taxman. Christopher so enjoys posting anything and everything anywhere it will fit. On one occasion the Skybox card was found under the sink in the kitchen and the best of it was he knew where he had put it. When asked if he knew its whereabouts he lead us straight to the cupboard, something we have found truly amazing. More often than not if the car keys go missing we just look behind the settee, sometimes finding everything except the kitchen sink. Now to the problem with the taxman. Having been a self employed driving instructor for twenty years it was perhaps no surprise when the business was chosen supposedly at random for an audit. Not a problem, we knew where everything was and all we had to do was take the lot over the tax office, attend their enquiry and that would be it. Wrong! It takes little working out that there should have been twenty diaries dating back to the eighties but there were only nineteen that could be found. You know the very one missing was for the year the audit was being conducted on and we were panicking. How could we justify our accounts without it, it was as good as a bible to a driving instructor and to the taxman.

To cut a long story short cast your mind back to a previous chapter, when Chris was on the Scamp project and he had been using the sun lounge as his classroom. At the same time as the diary had disappeared we were setting about redecorating the sun lounge and had decided to clear everything out of the way. Were we shocked when we pulled out a cupboard in the corner of the room, which had been there ever since Chris had been on the course?

13

There stuffed in behind the cupboard was the missing bible, sorry diary, together with all sorts of other things which we had written off months before as most probably having been put in the waste bin by Chris, another of his helpful ways. God Bless him!

Chapter 5
Christopher's Studio

"Where there's muck there's brass." That is quite a well-known saying in the north of England but down here in Southampton, in our home it took on a completely new meaning. It became obvious to us that Christopher's demands were increasing by the day and that both of us were needed to be around to control his outbursts. It was this, in January 2004, after much soul searching, that made our minds up that we should give up the driving school and concentrate on our other business which could be worked in the main whilst both boys were at school. You see we worked out that most pupils wanted driving lessons either in the evenings or at weekends, the very time Chris needed more of our attention. We have always thought that this decision was morally right, but of course it has had its financial implications, in our case it has been more muck, less brass. A case of cutting the cloth to suit if you like but somehow we have soldiered on in the face of all adversity.

We want to take you now into Christopher's studio, the place where every night he would spend hour after hour producing his wonderful masterpieces. We are of course referring to his bedroom but it was here that he would come up with something new nearly every night and sometimes more than once a night.

Before Chris was prescribed medication we had the Gods own task to get him settled at night and of course in the early days of his autism, it was so new to us that we were naive. Having put your child to bed you would expect them to perhaps lie awake for a little while and then drift off to sleep but we never had any such luck. Chris would never willingly stay in his room and so we decided a child gate across the door would do the trick. Wrong! In no time at all he had learnt to climb over it. Well, we thought, he definitely won't climb over two, one on top of the other. Wrong again, he could so he finished up with the two gates and then a piece of plywood over the top of these to stop his escape and even this didn't deter him some nights, as he would charge at the barrier and knock it down. Can you imagine how difficult it was for one or both of us to get into his room to check on him, sliding through that narrow opening? It's bad enough when there is only one gate but this meant being on all fours and crawling into the room.

Now let's get back to his artwork. We would watch him as closely as possible, remembering that some nights only one of us was available as the other was out trying to keep our business going, or spend time with our other son, Charlie. Chris was so clever that within minutes of your back being turned perhaps because you thought he was finally asleep, or because you had to attend to our other lad he would strip off, prepare what seemed to be a never ending supply of home made paint or clay, then spread it everywhere. Over the walls, over himself, his toys and of course over one of us when you tried to get him out of the room and down stairs to the bathroom. This happened so often that we quickly had a routine worked out, where one would clean Chris up and the other make sure that he had a clean canvas for his next lot of works. It is bad enough changing a baby but as a child grows so many of you will know so does the awful smell and of course the quantity.

With both of us having finished our tasks we would return Chris to his room and hope that we too might be able to settle down, maybe to watch a little telly or if the evening was getting on we might decide on going to bed. Great, a rest at last we would think until there it was again, his incessant screaming announcing that his next works were available for viewing.

No matter how tired you were it was a case of going through the cleaning processes again, whilst Christopher openly showed his approval. On one particular night he took great pride in helping. He offered his mum something and being the natural thing to do she accepted only to find she had in her hand some of his home produced modelling clay.

It might well be that even after two performances in one night he was not ready to settle down. He would just screech and screech whilst banging against the gates making sure we did not forget he was there. Some might think well why have the gates there in the first place but who knows what he may have done in the middle of the night had he had a free run of the house. God knows where he got his energy from but some nights the only way was for one of us to strap him in his car seat and take him for a drive, praying that it would not be too long before he dropped off, then would come the task of trying to get him back out of the car and safely into his bed once again, without waking him up. This process could take anything up to, and sometimes more than two hours driving, whilst singing lullabies. What a great way to spend a night and before you knew it our little human alarm would tell us it was time to get up again. Very often his screeching would start again by five am.

Not to be bored Christopher found other art forms that he could quite happily work on whilst in his room. One was smashing up his furniture. Pulling out drawers and jumping in them. Another pulling up the carpet only to reveal where he had already left his mark. Probably though, other than the smearing, the thing which we found so hard to believe was how night after night, again when we were out of sight he would use his bare hands, in fact his nails to dig away at and scrape off the paint from the walls. On one particular occasion when swept up it amounted to a full dustpan. He worked on this project until he had removed all the paint up as high as he could reach and then not to be beaten started digging away at the plaster.

The strange thing is, unlike any normal child, Chris did not seem to mind how much he plastered over himself in fact he revelled in it.

Always a big smile when you go into his room, even now, if he feels he has something to be proud of. It was suggested, by a nurse at the sleep clinic, who had been enlisted to help, that maybe he was deliberately covering himself to get the reward of a bath and that we should keep the cleaning up process as short as possible. Take away any toys from the bathroom, she told us, say as little as possible and return him to his room without stopping on the way.

Well, we tried all of this but to be fair it did not make any noticeable difference.

You need only be out of his room for a matter of minutes and upon your return you might find his night clothes torn up, nappy strewn across the room, faeces smeared everywhere and Chris himself looking like someone trying to do a retake of the black and white minstrels.

He will either stand there and laugh, waiting your reaction or now and then run and hide under what is left of his bedclothes, which leads us to believe he understands just how much it winds us up. At first it was terrible, just scrubbing, washing and cleaning up what others take for granted is sent down their sanitary systems. Now that waking, screeching, messing, cleaning process has become no more than a ritual to us, something we have to do so why moan, more often than not we get on with the job making sure we come up with something amusing to keep us from going under.

Chapter 6
Taking On Picasso

No matter how good Christopher's art had became we had to do something to stop it. We had to find some way where, having put him to bed, he would settle down, get to sleep and of course allow us to get some rest.

Bringing up any child is tiring but when you have one that starts his day anything from four thirty onwards and keeps going until past midnight it is a nightmare. No, it is not a nightmare it is hell. When day after day, night after night you have hardly any rest, barely any sleep it starts to take its toll. You do start to think why us? What have we done wrong to deserve this sentence? How long before one of us is ill?

We both can recall one time in particular. The driving school, although very successful over the years, was fast suffering because I was being called back home more and more often to help. It wasn't at night but a Saturday afternoon, when Chris had a really bad tantrum, charging about the room attacking anything in sight and all for no obvious reason. He was head butting the walls head butting the floor, biting himself and his brother Charlie. There was only one thing we came up with, to get him to his room where we had a better chance of containing his anger. Just getting him to his room was easier said than done but between us we struggled up the stairs with him and into his room, encouraging him to lie down on his bed.

There was absolutely no way he was going to calm down until he was ready. Every time we let go of him he would charge at the walls or hit out at one of us. It is a miracle that he didn't knock himself out or at the very least hurt himself. That afternoon seemed to last forever but eventually Chris called time on his anger and settled down. All we could do was look at each other, totally exhausted and cry.

Welcome to the world of an autistic child.

It was that same afternoon that the words of another of our customers came back to help us. A dear old lady had recently said to us "Always remember HIM UP THERE, pointing skyward, has chosen you to be special parents. Special children need a special mum and dad and don't you forget it.

Thinking of those words of wisdom helped us to wipe away the tears that day and to think of something positive. Something that we hoped would at least reduce the amount of time Chris spent on his art and encourage him to get a good nights sleep. Perhaps our new idea might prove to be successful. We decided that we would take it in turns to lay down with him when we took him to bed and stay there until he had settled. Many is the night when we fell asleep before he did but at least it put the brakes on for a while. Of course whilst we might have stopped the early evening performance it did not stop Chris from waking later that same night or maybe even earlier than usual the next morning and catching up on his work. That meant for us it was back to scrubbing duties.

It put a whole new meaning to the saying about a night on the tiles. With Chris more often than not covered, it always meant two baths, one to get the worst off and another to sweeten him up as unfortunately at that time we had no shower facilities.

With this particular habit came another really nasty problem, one that prevented my oldest son Brian, who was still living at home at that time, from bringing any friends indoors. We completely understood when he told us he was embarrassed to have his mates around because the house stunk.

He was absolutely right for no matter how many bottles and cans of disinfectant and air freshener we used the smell never seemed to go away. With the paint off the walls in Christopher's room all of his smearing soaked into the plaster and no matter how hard you scrubbed you could still smell the after affects as soon as you walked in the front door.

For one reason or another we had never really had a high regard for social workers but it was during this period, when probably we felt at our wits end that we decided we had to take some positive steps forward. We were not going to solve our problems all on our own we needed help. After talking to our health visitor and making some enquiries of our own we were appointed a social worker from the team for disabled children. All we had to do then was wait for the first visit, could it be that our prayers were to be answered?

Chapter 7
Our Angel Arrives

Finally, the moment arrived, the day we were to meet a young lady who would perhaps start to turn our lives around. When she arrived, Kelly, as she introduced herself, was so full of bounce and vigour she made us feel not only at ease but installed belief that she and her team could help us see that light at the end of the tunnel. We were able to talk openly to Kelly and soon realised that whilst she could not always answer every question on the spot she would find out the answer and let us know. Unlike many professionals who seem evasive, she would tackle everything head on, quickly realising that we had a genuine reason to ask for her help.

One of her greatest concerns was to check that we were getting all of the financial help that we were entitled to and secondly to help us with the safety and health issues around the home and in particular within Christopher's room. By this time he had broken one of his bedroom windows and some glass in the kitchen door both by head butting them miraculously without cutting himself. Not to be left out though Charlie had made sure he rubbed his head on the bedroom window and had brought blood from his forehead. By the time Kelly got to see Christopher's room we had fitted some of that plastic garden netting over his window to avoid a recurrence. His room looked nothing short of a mess, not through our neglect but by his insistence to keep up his daily rituals. We had a social worker who was genuinely stunned; at last this vibrant young person was lost for words.

Lost for words but not for ideas. She told us that one hundred per cent effort would be put in to help improve our family's quality of life. Kelly could see that if something was not done quickly with Christopher's room there could be serious repercussions. She told us she was going to contact the occupational therapist and enlist her help in solving the problem. When we asked how long this process might take knowing that one normally waits weeks sometime months for health professionals to fit you in Kelly assured us it would not be long. True to her word and her insistence Kelly made sure the occupational therapist, another very understanding young lady, was out to our home in little over two weeks.

Kelly had already warned her what to expect but we will never forget the look on her face when she arrived at the top of our stairs. There, right in front of her, were those prison gates and just like we did several times each day she had to get down and crawl inside. Shock, horror, amazement, all were written on Vicky's face and like Kelly on her first visit she really did not know what to say. After making notes and asking us what we thought would be the answer the idea was put forward to have a "SAFE SPACE" created within Christopher's room. A safe space, that sounded good but what exactly was it and how would we pay for something like that.

These two young ladies had the answers. We were told that a Safe Space was a room built within another with soft sides that would be easily washable and a secure door meaning we wouldn't have to worry about those blasted gates ever again. As to the cost it was suggested that we apply for a grant and both ladies confirmed they would support our application.

As the two ladies prepared to leave us the occupational therapist said that what she had seen, and knowing the efforts we had made to keep the room clean had brought her close to tears. We know she was closer than she thought and we firmly believe we are just two of the few that have actually seen tears roll down a professional's cheek. We were so lucky that young lady was assigned to our case, we knew like the social worker she was on our side and was prepared to give her all to help, perhaps we had been granted two guardian angels.

Chapter 8
The Knock On Effects

At this stage it is worth remembering that we had been told by the Paediatrician that Christopher was one of the most severe cases of autism she had encountered throughout her long career. It was going to take something special to turn our fortunes around.

It was also clear that little Charlie had been affected by his brother's actions and we had to make sure that he was allowed to lead as normal a life as possible. We had already survived two major frights with Charlie, the first being meningitis when we thought we might lose him and the second when he sustained a double break in his arm after an accident. Unless you have been in the position it is difficult to imagine what it feels like when it is touch and go with your child's life.

It became more and more obvious that Charlie was perhaps being affected, or perhaps a better word might be influenced, by his younger brother's behaviour, mimicking some of the sounds and actions. Some of the things he has done have added to the pressure upon us but having thought long and hard about it we have decided not to go into too much detail about those. So that you fully realise that we had two difficult children to look after we will just scratch the surface. The paediatrician, like us, knew he had some problems and he was eventually diagnosed with emotional and behavioural disorder. It was obviously deemed to affect us enough as Charlie too was awarded DLA. Charlie, still to this day has some problems, but not academically, he is doing very well. It is obvious that now having turned ten years Charlie is beginning to understand more how this whole thing affects us as a family. Charlie's love of animals has been instrumental in him being determined to become a vet one day and various things make us think this is possible, perhaps one in particular, his brilliance at mental arithmetic, another his knowledge on wildlife captured by his habitual reading on the subject. We are confident that Charlie will make something special of his life. Let me tell you if he makes it there will not be another veterinary surgeon who will have as much feeling for their patients.

It has always been difficult to spend time with Charles, he hates us calling him that, or to take him out on trips and try explaining to a young lad why he couldn't be like other kids his age and have friends round to play. The truth is we were embarrassed. For sure, one could not hide that awful smell that lingered no matter what remedial miracles you had performed. Smearing, that you had missed, perhaps on a wall or over some of the toys, it was almost impossible to keep up with cleaning. As you read on through the book you will find out that there are days when things have not changed too much. We were worried about what children might say to their parents or perhaps taunt Charlie when they were at school. More than once he has come home and said no one believes he has an autistic brother. Fine, kids that age don't really understand, but Charlie being a bright little spark was hurt by such suggestions.

"Never mind Charlie," I told him, "One day those same so called friends may be haunted by actions as a child. When they grow up and have children some of them may have autistic children of their own."

His chance came to prove to his peers he had been telling the truth when the local paper ran yet another article on Christopher and Charlie lost little time in taking it in to show everyone. Whether his peers completely understood is not sure but I believe it put the troops on the back foot for a while.

It had not been the first time the Parker's had hit the news, not just the news but also the headlines. There had been problems when, as I mentioned earlier, Charlie injured his arm, aged four and it was not until a check up a week after the accident that the doctors discovered the true extent of the damage. Damage that would need immediate surgery to bring the bones back into line but surgery through one reason and another that took over twenty four hours to organise throughout which time our little chap was refused food or drink.

That's right, a full day waiting, nil by mouth, just because someone had lost his notes and during which time we were subjected to waiting in a corridor, there being no bed available. Charlie was in enormous pain but we, his parents had to buy pain-killing medicine from downstairs apparently because no one had yet taken responsibility for his care. The only way we moved things forward was to contact the local rag and the story made front page.

As a family we do not do things by half. Lets take you back even further when Charlie was still only a few months old and we were both out at work on this particular Friday evening with Anna and Brian both at home babysitting. At this time we had a beautiful boxer bitch and on that evening she was laid across the patio door opening when Brian noticed it had started to rain.

Knowing there were clothes on the line he decided to bring them in but as he went past the dog he tripped. God knows what made her turn but she absolutely savaged the backs of Brian's legs and the poor little lads private parts and it was only the bravery of his sister that probably saved him from further harm. It was a case of blue lights and straight into resuscitation on arrival at hospital.

Thank the Lord and those hospital staff who saved his life. This incident not only made the local news but the nationals and gave television their headlines. We shall never forget the torment we received from the media with TV crews trying to film the inside of our home through the windows whilst we were at the hospital and when we had left to come home some joker tried to gain access to the ward by saying he was a relative.

Suddenly, as if by fate, we were relegated to the inside pages as it was the weekend that the world lost one of its most treasured ladies,

Princess Diana. Incidentally it was also the weekend of Charlie's Christening but that went ahead and Brian insisted on coming home to take his place in the Church, such was his courage and bravery.

You must understand how these moments in our lives have indeed affected us all, not only as individuals but as a family. So many tears have been shed, so many worrying times, perhaps more than our fair share yet thankfully through our unity, care and love for each other we have all survived to tell the tale.

It is of course little Charlie, as he grows up who finds it most difficult to take on board how different our lives are compared to those of his friends. Instead of playing with his mates very often, Charlie continues to extend his knowledge of his great loves, animals and nature. Reading adult books such as Readers Digest and watching programmes like David Attenborough's nature stories has meant that he has become almost an authority on the subject. It is wonderful to listen to him spill out all the facts and figures on all sorts of creatures. His caring nature shows through when he is out with his rabbits, all so tame thanks to his time and energy. You can't beat a bit of rabbit pie but try telling him that, they are an extension to the family.

Chapter 9
Help Wasn't The Word

Enough of digressing let us get back to those angels, or more to, the point what they had started. As we said earlier we were worried about the funding for improvements on Christopher's room and if it had been all down to us there would have been a major set back, money by this time was tight.

We had been told by the occupational therapist to contact the grants department of the Southampton City Council with a view to them helping with the cost. Help! Help wasn't the word! We shall always be indebted to the gentleman and his department who took on our case. We are pretty sure that neither he nor his department will mind us mentioning his name, as it is our way of showing our gratitude in public. One hears of so many people who never have a good word to say about grants officers but it is hardly surprising some people get turned down, either because they are blatantly rude or because they try to cheat the system. We actually read of someone who had applied for a grant for new windows and when the grants officer entered the property he could see it was in good order.

He was also bemused at why the lounge was virtually empty except for chairs around its perimeter and certainly shocked when looking around the rest of the property realised it was in fact a brothel and that the madam was extremely rich. She apparently complained when turned down but should she have tried to fiddle the system? Does it not make it harder for genuine applicants?

Let us make it clear that providing you are honest and polite your application will be looked at fairly. Mr Andy Walker, that was the man, who deserves all the thanks we can bestow upon him. Such a modest person and a gentleman who looked at our case in a fair and just way. Like the Angels, he too was horror-stricken when he saw what Christopher had done to his room, what we had to try to keep clean. Being a rather portly gentleman, sorry Mr Walker, we removed the child gates, once he had seen them in place, in order that he could assess the full extent of the problem. On entering he was able to see just how hard it was to not only keep clean but also to make sure it was hygienic. Where Christopher had scraped the paint off the walls and then smeared on them it was extremely hard to guarantee any hygiene at all. With the plaster exposed and being a porous material his faeces became more and more embedded and obviously more difficult to remove. Being on a tight budget meant luxuries like rubber gloves were not an option so by the time one had finished the cleaning you had to scrub like mad to get the stench off of you. The stench, smell, whatever one called it, would not go away and probably was one of the major factors that helped win the day.

Together with the occupational therapist, who had met him at our home they discussed the situation and swapped ideas on possible solutions? Eventually it was decided that perhaps a SAFE SPACE would be the answer. Something that would contain Chris and at the same time keep him safe and so there it was, the answer, all we had to do now was contact the company that erected these safe spaces and all our troubles were over.

We discovered much to our horror that this safe space was to cost around £4,500 but without hesitation permission was granted to go ahead. Measurements were taken of Chris's "L" shaped room and sent off to the company, whilst we sat back and awaited with anticipation the answer to all our prayers. Finally we got the phone call. We'll be there tomorrow to fit the safe space; it'll take us about an hour and a half.

Now this is where we smelt a rat. An hour and a half, to totally transform that disgusting room, it didn't seem possible. Fortunately Chris was in respite so we were able to strip out the room, scrub it clean and await the big moment. That was a major task itself, tearing up carpet that had been urinated on night after night, treating the floorboards with a very strong disinfectant, waiting for that to dry and then painting on a waterproof floor paint. In truth that whole exercise took us well into the night but although very late we had to take a couple of baths each before we felt any where near clean enough to retire to our bed. Perhaps some of you are thinking why did they leave the carpet down and allow it to become so bad, why hadn't they done something more about it. Let us make it clear that in total three different carpets had been fitted in that room from the time Christopher started his antics up to the arrival of the safe space. It really was a case of swallowing pride for the last two carpets were ones we managed to get for free one from a friend, another from an understanding customer.

Although we had been up late preparing Christopher's room we still had to be about early in anticipation of our miracle arriving. The morning dragged on into early afternoon and still no one had arrived so we decided to ring the company and make sure we had got it right. "Yes", they said, they are on the way, just got a little bit lost.

Finally a van arrived and out stepped two women and our first thoughts, without being sexist, how the hell are they going to be able to do this job. Do it they did but it was not what we were expecting, was this it, for four and a half grand? For a start it did not fit the shape of the room and secondly it really was nothing more than a very expensive tent. There was a door opening and window both of which were secured by a zip fastener but there was one obvious problem to us straight away, there was a clasp both on the outside and the inside which meant that the person inside would be able to open up whenever they wished. One of the ladies told us that she had an autistic son and that he slept in one of these spaces and was quite happy, only time would tell if this was the answer to our problems.

At least now we had a secure place for Christopher to sleep, somewhere that meant we could rest easy, wash the sides fairly easily as one thing that did not stop was his constant smearing. As far as Christopher was concerned he had just been moved to a new studio and he was going to make dam sure that it was soon home from home. He also made sure that on quite a few nights of the week he gave more than one performance. With the frustration of being imprisoned his screeching seemed to become progressively worse and his physical aggression likewise. It was not long, perhaps a couple of months that we noticed he was able, when in the so called safe space, to charge the sides of it and slowly but surely move it across the room until he was close enough to the wall outside to head butt it. What were we to do? Having spent many nights in the old environment trying to prevent him from self harming and perhaps not smearing we thought that we might have more time to ourselves. Did these new developments mean that we were back to square one?

Something else had also happened. Chris had discovered that the transparent material used in the window was not impenetrable. One could see more and more marks appearing as a result of constant digging with his nails and it was not long before he had managed to break through in places. It was quite obvious it was only a matter of time before he made these small holes much larger. If the situation had not been addressed quickly we would either have had an escapee or a son with a badly battered head. We were not prepared to accept either of these possibilities.

The grants officer had told us when he came to check the safe space on instalment that if we had any problems we were to contact him without any hesitation. For sure, he did not expect us to take up his offer after such a short time but we once again needed help.

Chapter 10
Our Ace Comes Up Trumps

In life you are dealt your cards and you have to play them the best way you can, you can't hand them back, you cannot change them. How you play those cards is up to you, your attitude, your determination and your desire to win. Some of our cards represent our children and no matter what problems they have there is absolutely no way we would want to be without them. Of course everyone who plays cards hopes to be dealt some aces. As far as we were concerned we had to wait for a long time for an ace to be dealt our way but it turned up just at the right time. Have you guessed? The Ace that made a difference in our lives came in the form of our grants officer.

It is true to say that before his intervention we were pretty desperate. Night after night having very little sleep, a house that constantly stunk no matter how much we struggled to clean, no matter how many tins of air freshener we went through, it was yet another period of life in hell. Then for a few brief moments, in reality some three to four months, of our lives we were back in heaven, when the safe space was first installed, only to find we were heading straight back to hell. Desperate again, we rang Mr Walker and explained the situation, how Christopher had showed in his own practical way that the Safe Space was not the answer. Straight away his answer was one of re-assurance, telling us not to worry, he would see us the next day and that he would do his best to sort out the problem.

True to his word the following day the grants officer was out to see us and without hesitation agreed that a mistake had been made, the safe space was not the answer. So if that wasn't the answer what was going to do the job? Well this is where my wife Tina came into her own. She had made some preliminary investigations on the Internet and found a company called TFS. There was no need for delay, Tina told Mr Walker of her findings and wasted no time at all in logging on to their web site. Their site showed examples of fully padded rooms, none of this tent business, just wall to wall padding and with options to have sensory or play panels built into the design. Well said the grants officer, get them on the phone when you have time and invite them down. "When we had time." Once Mr Walker had said his goodbyes I was given the phone number and assigned the task of contacting TFS. What worried us was how much it might be, bearing in mind the safe space had been £4,500 and even worse, would we be expected to pay the bill?

There was nothing we could do other than wait for the representative from TFS to arrive and provide the dreaded quote. When after a couple of weeks the gentleman turned up and met with us, the occupational therapist and Mr Walker we were all truly amazed at his proposals to transform the bedroom into somewhere that Christopher would not only be safe but also have provision for things that would stimulate him and perhaps detract, for at least some of the time, from his bad habits. Not being drawn into guessing a price the TFS man promised after taking the necessary measurements to ring us within two days with the quote.

Well, were we surprised, when the quotation arrived, comparing what had been paid for the previous effort £7,500 did not seem so bad. Bearing in mind that the work included a fully padded floor, padded walls from floor to ceiling, which included a special soft "Blackboard", an area where Velcro toys could be stuck, inserts within the padding on another wall where a padded Butterfly, Ladybird, Snail and Bee could be pushed in or removed as took Christopher's fancy.

Of course the big worry now was whether the local authority would accept responsibility for the bill. Although very anxious and worried we need not have been because much to our relief we were given the green light. It was just a case now of saying, "When can you start?"

In fairness it was not long at all and when the two fitters arrived they quickly demonstrated their professionalism finishing what was an absolutely wonderful job in five and a half days, some difference to the one and a half hours to pitch the tent.

With the involvement of the grants team came many more benefits for they had been assessing our plight and new that other parts of the house needed urgent attention to assure Christopher's safety. Toughened glass was fitted in to all windows that Christopher was able to reach and head butt, he had already broken two by this method. Bomb proof film was fitted both inside and out on our sun lounge windows and this has always raised a laugh when we have told people we have a ready made bunker in case of war. In both our downstairs bathroom and shower room upstairs work was desperately needed. You may ask why it hadn't been done but the truth of the matter is we could not afford it, money was tight, remember we had been forced, through circumstance, to relinquish one full time income.

There was a leak somewhere within the shower upstairs, one which had already resulted in the lounge ceiling being brought down, so that had been marked out of bounds for months, which meant when Christopher performed we had to guide him all the way downstairs and do the double bath routine. Without boring you too much it was agreed that both these vitally essential rooms have a complete make over and now we have the luxury of a shower upstairs and down. All we were asked to do was contribute a reasonable amount towards the work one of the bathrooms.

Controlling Christopher, or stopping him running riot about the home was also a big issue. We had fitted something like a stable door on the divide between lounge and kitchen just to keep the little devil out of the danger zone but Chris was having none of this. At every opportunity he would charge the door until one day he took the whole lot off of the wall, hinges and all. So what was Mr Walker and his team's answer? They not only repaired that particular wall and fitted a much stronger door; they went right through the home with new doors, each with a lock and key, so that we could at last keep Chris where we wanted him. Yes, sometimes it does seem like one is living in a prison but better that than our son be a constant threat to his own safety.

All this work, all this help, it made us feel very humble, that someone had finally seen and recognised many of our problems. Even down to an air conditioning unit being fitted in the boys bedrooms when, after a few months and with summer temperatures soaring temperatures went well over 100 degrees farenheight.

Even the Safe Space didn't go to waste as it was agreed to move this into little Charlie's room, he to having his problems.

Of course fitting this padded room and doing all of these improvements did not make Christopher's autism go away, neither has it stopped him to this day, carrying on with his art work but it sure has made it easier to clean his canvases and make ready for his next performance. Gone too have much of the lingering smells, just those now as and when he presents a new piece of work. Without doubt the worst thing about going into his room these days is that he has taken to using the artex ceiling as an extra canvas. Neither is it just the effort trying to clean the ceiling, moreover the surprise you get from aerial attacks, when lumps of his masterpiece give in to gravity.

One thing is for sure the Ace Card we had been dealt had proved invaluable; one could say it had turned out to be our trump card!

Chapter 11

Out And About

How often do you say to your partner "Lets take the kids out?" How often do you say to the kids, "Come on let's go to the park" or "Let's go for a swim?"

For most those simple pleasures can be taken for granted but for the many thousands out there who have severely autistic children and for us it's a nightmare. In the early days of Christopher's autistic life he wasn't too bad and we were able to go out here and there for treats or perhaps enjoy the simple pleasure of both man and wife going out together to do the shopping, all of which is now totally impossible. In an earlier chapter we told how Chrissy had bitten his brother whilst we were in Tescos and then proceeded to scream the place down. That was really embarrassing, enduring the stares from fellow customers, many of which probably thought we were useless parents but you know what, we would give anything to go into Tescos these days with both of our sons, even if we were stared at as if we were aliens. It would be such a treat just to take a fit in our head and say let's go in that place for a bite to eat. The closest we get to McDonalds is through the drive through and even then we have to apologise for Christopher's impatient screaming.

The arrival of a buggy helped the situation a little, giving him space in which he felt a little more comfortable but one still had to be careful where you went. A few instances come to mind, one in particular proving to be very embarrassing.

We had taken the two boys along to Charlie's infant school for their annual firework display, deciding the walk would do us good we left the car at home. All wrapped up warm off we went and all was well until we encountered the crowds that had gathered for the display. Christopher became more and more agitated and was clearly going to let everyone around know just what his feelings were, starting his screeching in direct competition with the "Wiz Bangs" of the fireworks. Standing close to us was a dear little girl who would insist on gradually getting closer and closer to Chris in his buggy. He was having none of it, no one was invading his space and with our eyes on the display he took the opportunity to kick the girl right in the head. Now there were two screaming kids, with us having to be as humble as possible and apologise to the girl's parents.

As the autism has got worse, Christopher has become more and more challenging when it comes to going somewhere new and in fact whether at school or at home he now has to have two to one care.

Just a short while ago we desperately needed a few bits in town and decided as Charlie was at school we would try our luck and take Christopher so we could both make decisions on what we should buy. No Chance! In the first instance it took both of us to transfer him from the car to his buggy.

He was having none of it and after walking probably no more than fifty yards from the car we had to turn back, one of us staying in the car with Chris whilst the other ran round to the shop, grabbed what was needed and ran back. Throughout those one hundred yards we would have been dead and buried many times if looks could have killed. In fact it is surprising that nobody rang the police or social services, perhaps it was just the entertainment value they were assessing.

Another attempt to get him out in the community was a visit to the shoe shop to get his feet measured, a pretty simple task for normal parents, but one for us that could easily have resulted in a lawsuit. Not too bad this time getting out of the car and pushing him in the buggy just a few yards to the shop but what happened when we got inside was totally different. Chris went absolutely mad, kicked the footrest off of the buggy, launching it several feet across the room and hitting this dear old lady just above the ankle. How do you get out of that one? Easy, offer your sincere apologies, tell her Chris is autistic, listen to her going on and then make a speedy retreat, knowing that what you had said had gone in one ear, straight out the other and that in her opinion we were just terrible parents. To this day we have not had Christopher's feet measured, we just buy what we think is right, take them home and try them on and repeat the process until we find the right ones.

Let's take the opportunity to tell you about visiting my sister and her husband, again something taken for granted by thousands, but for us yet another strain on the nerves as we wonder what he will break this time. One of the problems is that Doreen, that's aunty Daw Daw to Chris, has a Jack Russell puppy and although it is shut in the front room when we arrive Christopher knows it is there and has to be carried, sometimes almost dragged by both of us from the car to the house. Once at the back door it is a mad dash for a carver chair, which he climbs up on, and perches, precariously balanced on the arm and back and that is where he stays for most of the visit, demanding jelly and cakes. An even worst problem is that my sister is mad on collecting ornaments and every shelf on the welsh dresser and the windowsills are littered with these very attractive missiles. No matter how one tries to concentrate on Christopher and watch what his eyes are beaming in on it is impossible to guarantee their safety. He is just so quick and very, very clever. The minute he notices you have been distracted he will grab something, launch it down the other end of the room and then laugh. Of course he is waiting for a reaction and try as you might to play his actions down sometimes this proves impossible. He is just so quick that even if you do spot what he is up to you just cannot move fast enough yourself to prevent the deed. If he can't find anything to throw he might resort to tipping the dregs from a teacup or on his way out kick over the dog's water bowl. Is it any wonder that we do not visit our relatives that often these days?

How embarrassing for his mum when she took him into Woolworth's. It was not long after we had been given the buggy and before his risk assessment was updated showing he required two to one care at all times.

Just a simple walk around shop, whilst I popped to the bank next door; or was it? Chris saw his chance, grabbed a beautiful glass vase and sent it crashing to the floor. It has to be said that the staff in Woolworth's were so understanding even when Chris gave them his celebratory smile. It must have been one of the hastiest retreats anyone has made from that store.

As you have already gathered Dogs and Christopher do not go together, something we are usually so careful about but one Sunday not so long back we slipped up badly. Sunday afternoon is occasionally a time where we buck up courage, find some spare bread and venture out to feed the ducks. Now most times this little outing goes off without too much bother, a few screams and a bit of kicking. That's when we can park very close to a duck pond that is completely fenced in and from which dogs are barred but this particular Sunday there was a change of plan. We would not go to usual place, rather to a local river, alongside which ran a nice straight path where little Charlie could ride his scooter. Have you guessed? As soon as we were out of the car with Chris in his buggy, every dog owner in Hampshire seemed to arrive on the same stretch of river. Christopher started screeching, shaking back and forth in the buggy drawing yet again an extremely large audience. There was nothing else we could do but return to the car, Christopher still screeching and little Charlie upset that he had not been able to take his ride. That particular occasion it took well over an hour for him to calm down, lashing out and kicking the back of the driver's seat all the way home and remonstrating until a bath seemed to do the trick. All of this was because as parents we changed venues just because we knew there would be an ice cream van along the riverbank.

Just one last little example of how difficult going out can be for us all. Christopher had been going fortnightly to a little club run by a charity named Kidz and at Christmas time all of the children together with their siblings and parents were invited to a party. Having just had shoulder surgery it was difficult for me to help keep Christopher under control and he quickly worked out that by staying at the back of the bouncy castle it would be difficult for his mum to do anything either. With a push and a smack he had a little girl on the floor and was attacking her leaving Tina with no option but to climb onto the bouncy castle and try to rescue the girl. In no time at all he had his mum on the deck as well and she had to put every ounce of effort into getting up and pulling him away from the equipment. Strangely there were none of the club's helpers who took up the challenge or who offered their help. From the time we arrived to our departure we had spent twenty nerve-racking minutes trying in vain to enjoy ourselves.

It would be so easy to go on and on about attempts to go out but you know it is not just us that have the problems. At school Chris is exactly the same, willing to a degree to get into the mini bus but flatly refusing to get out with the other children at the destination.

After so many extraordinary experiences it is clear to us that we must accept the need for us to live within Christopher's boundaries. Gone are the days, at least for the immediate future, when we can make an on the spot decision to go somewhere. Come to think of it, almost gone are the days when we dare to plan anything in advance because no matter how much thought is put into the planning that particular dream can be shattered in a moment.

Chapter 12
The World Through A Glass Window

Having taken in the last chapter you will probably have come to the same conclusion as us, that when Christopher is not at school, we become virtual prisoners within our four walls of our home.

That is unless we decide to take a look at the world outside through a glass window. So what do I mean? When Christopher is at home and I must emphasise here that we love him being with us, he is such an important part of our family, the only way we can go out anywhere is to window shop from the car.

When we chose our Vauxhall Zafira it was done so with Christopher and his habits very much in mind. Before life with the seven seater Chris would travel in the rear seats of my driving school car, a Peugeot 205 and would kick out at me whilst I was driving. Having been granted mobility allowance allowed us to buy the Zafira, which we hoped would be the answer to so many problems but how wrong could we be?

We could not put Chris in the very back seats because he was then too close to the window and enjoyed either head butting, banging it with his fist or hitting it with his toys. So it had to be the centre of the middle row and hope that kicking the driver would soon be a thing of the past. Now there arose another problem because as Christopher's autism grew worse so did his acceptance of anyone sitting next to him. Many is the time Tina has been in the seat next to him and he has suddenly attacked her, pulling her beautiful long hair or biting her. We were told to turn away when he had one of these tantrums, try to ignore it but that is so much easier said than done. The trouble was that if he had no one sat next to him he would constantly undo his seat belt and have free range as to where he moved, obviously this could not go on, as it was extremely dangerous.

Once again it was Tina's ingenuity and knowledge of the Internet that came to the rescue. She had spoken to various people and discovered on the net a company that specialised in safety harnesses for the disabled. Sorted, except that we were told there were no funds available to have the harness purchased for us and so we forked out the eighty-seven pounds for this top of the range equipment, which he could never get out of on his own. The Houdini it was called. It should be Christopher that is called by that name, because after only just a few months he was able to undo the harness faster than we could release our own seat belts. There was one advantage in as much that whilst it was secure he could not reach to kick me but that all changed as his legs grew longer and he quickly made up for lost time If something upset him he would lash out repeatedly, kicking me and sometimes Tina in the passenger seat, as hard as he could.

My left shoulder in particular was taking the brunt of his attacks and it was more by accident that I discovered my shoulder had been broken and healed in the wrong place. I was at the hospital to see a specialist about my tennis elbow and when asked how it was I told the gentleman that compared to my shoulder pain it was nothing.

His answer was to send me for an x-ray on the damaged shoulder, which confirmed it had in deed been broken. Without wasting too much of your time let me just tell you that it took over a year and two wrongly arranged appointments with the elbow guy again before I finally found myself in front of the shoulder consultant. After another year I have recently had corrective surgery, which to perfectly honest has done little to ease the pain. Christopher still gives me a timely reminder if the pain starts to ease.

One of my biggest problems is that I digress, forgive me I will get back to story. By this time Kerry Dixon our social worker had moved on and you might well know the old saying "After the Lord Mayor's show"…Well we had Kelly's replacement and quickly asked for her to be replaced and then our case notes were handed to a gentleman named Nigel, Our new Social worker. Worker he proved to be for it was only after a few meetings with him and the discovery of our problem that he promised to contact different companies and charities with a view to them funding protective screens behind each of the front seats. Mind, it might well have been the fact that he came to the school with me one afternoon to pick Christopher up and as soon as we pulled away from the school he felt a toy whistle past his ear. Good on you Chris, right on cue.

"Fantastic", I shouted, as Nigel announced he had been successful in his quest. We were to get two shields, costing seven hundred pounds; just like the police and taxi drivers have to protect them. Chris would never be able to throw another thing towards us, never again would he be able to kick me whilst I was driving. I could imagine my shoulder giving a sigh of relief.

Sigh it might, but suffer it still would, for in Christopher's eyes the screens were like red rag to a bull, taking every opportunity to kick out with all his worth. Now when Chris gets in the car one of the first things he does is to remove his shoes and socks, so please remember he was doing most of the kicking with his bare feet. After about three months I called the social worker and he was astounded when I told him that Christopher had broken my shield almost right the way across. "Don't worry," he said, "That one must be faulty, I will get it replaced." Fine, he got it replaced but let me tell you that within another few months Christopher had broken that as well. Does it not make you worry for the safety of our law enforcers or our taxi drivers or could it just be that Christopher has incredible strength? The company who supplied the shields did not know what to do next, neither did our social worker but I did, promptly removing them for

Christopher's safety as they had broken jagged edges on which he could cut his feet.

You probably already get the picture that going out for us is not much fun, moreover something that you do because you feel you have to try. You look at so many other families who are able to go out and enjoy themselves; boy does it make you envious sometimes?

As Chris got older and consequently longer in the leg he discovered a new entertainment or skill. He found he was able to wind the windows down using his feet and on more than one occasion followed up by throwing something out of the window.

One particular time could have been extremely dangerous as he had quite a large toy he was playing with that day and having wound the window down proceeded to throw the toy out on to the motorway.

Fortunately it got stuck or it could have caused a serious accident. Our response to this was to go to the Vauxhall garage and have them remove the winders from each of the rear doors so now if we want a window down a little bit we use a pair of pliers. Problem is Christopher has to have the last word it would seem on everything and now chooses to kick the hell out of the windows. I just wonder how long they can take it before they shatter.

Apart from his legs getting longer so have his arms and Chris has discovered he can make it pretty difficult for the driver if he grabs their seat belt and pulls on it as hard as possible. It really is a dangerous distraction when you feel yourself being choked knowing you cannot take your eyes off the road, or hands off the wheel. Tina has come to my rescue or more than one occasion.

You tell me, how would most people feel if they were out for a nice drive in the countryside, and suddenly a piece of wet nappy or a lump of faeces whizzed past your ear or hit you in the back of the head? Could you put up with your child screeching from the time you set out on your journey right up until you returned home. Is it any wonder that sometimes we are only out for a very short time?

On one occasion recently we were out for a drive and remembered we needed a couple of things for the boys. Instead of going home first I suggested we go straight to Tescos and that Tina wait in the car with the boys whilst I popped in to the shop. I don't suppose I was gone for more than twenty minutes but on return to the car saw Tina stood outside whilst Christopher was still in his harness but had torn his clothes completely off, his modesty saved only by his Houdini. Tina explained that Charlie and her had got out of the car to take a rest from the screeching and as we were talking some ignorant woman shouted to us to get back in the car and have our conversation so she could have our space. I will not disclose what I told her other than to make it clear that Christopher had problems and for once we carried on and finished what we were talking about leaving this woman to become more and more infuriated. Wow! Was this road rage I had started?

There are of course times when Christopher is calmer in the car and we enjoy those moments to the full but it can only take a second, some minute change in procedure, to kick him off into a tantrum. Some of the things we have done to combat his screeching and tantrums include turning the music up very loud on the radio and once he realises he is not being heard he gives up.

Another more recent method is to endorse one of his fairly new habits that of taking stickers from a sheet and making pictures on a piece of card. Until the introduction of a sand timer, which gives Chris a conception of time, this proved pretty expensive but one proved money well spent. Of course it can have its negative affects if we run out of stickers in the car, then he starts up his screaming or shouting for more.

Other damage he has done to the interior of the car includes, breaking the overhead light, smashing the rear air vents with his feet and biting holes in the headrests. One the most repulsive things is when he constantly wets on the seats, having been taken to the toilet just before being put into the car. Another is unloading his pants or nappy and smearing it all over the seats.

How when we have a car like this can we offer anyone a lift, it feels awful on a rainy day having to drive past an elderly neighbour for fear of being embarrassed. Chris is getting a little better in this department but we still find ourselves having to scrub the inside clean on a very regular basis.

It is not just our car that suffers, he does a fair amount of damage to the school mini bus but before concluding this chapter let me tell what happened with his school escorts for he saw two of them off in a matter of weeks. The first gave up after Chris bit her on both arms, through quite a thick coat, and left her with a bruise on each arm the size of a digestive biscuit. The transport at that time was an ordinary taxi and even the driver was worried sick as to whether his car would survive the journey unscathed. The Educational transport department then thought they had the answer. On our advice they bought a new and updated harness and would use a mini bus to transport him to and fro. Well the harness worked fine but they hadn't foreseen that Chris was sat close enough to head butt the windows. His escort, apparently a very experienced lady in this field was to be Christopher's next victim. She put her arm between Chris and the window to prevent him breaking it and he obliged by biting her on the arm and when she went to the front of him to try again he kicked her in the face. Exit school transport, for the next we heard was from the educational transport department pleading for us to take him to school ourselves for a couple of weeks whilst they resolved the problem and found a new escort. Well I don't suppose too many of you are surprised when I tell you that we are still doing the job for them. What's more I bet we will never hear from that department again.

Chapter 13
Holiday Hell!

Most people who are fortunate to have holidays each year at some time or other will come home and tell everyone they have had a Holiday from Hell. Generally this is a one off and the remainder of their vacations run pretty smoothly. What I would say to those folks and indeed anyone who has been able to take regular holidays throughout their lives, lucky you.

If you have been fortunate to take at least one break a year, there are those who have more, then spare a thought for the people who through no fault of their own have not been so lucky. Not just people like our selves but the many millions throughout civilisation that cannot do so because they are caring for children, or adults, with a severe disability. It quite likely is not their financial situation that stops them booking a break, but moreover the sheer worry of coping with the person in their charge or perhaps the inability to find someone else willing to look after their child whilst they are away.

Let me tell you about our last real holiday, taken as a family, some four years ago when we thought it would be perfectly safe to take Christopher with us to Gran Canaria. From the outset we knew from experience that Chris would not cope well with waiting for too long in queues so we made it our business when we booked the flights to explain our situation to the airline. Not a problem was their immediate response, just head for the front of the booking in queue, tell us who you are and we will do the rest. It sounded great but how many times have you heard promises like this, only to find in reality there was little or no help whatsoever.

We had to struggle on our own, through baggage handling, customs and boarding the plane and it was only as we were stepping on to the aircraft and a hostess heard me complaining that we were given any assistance. We had to touch down at Lanzarotti to pick up more passengers and during this break in the flight we had one hell of a job on our hands. We had to get Christopher to the back of the plane, into the cramped toilet and change his nappy. Believe me he went absolutely wild, screaming and kicking all the way along the aircraft. No help was offered here, neither was there any sympathy when they told us the children must have adult meals as there were none provided for them.

That little bit of help as we boarded was followed by an assurance that the same would not happen on the return journey. They were right there, it was worse. No consideration was given to us, even though Christopher was screaming as loud as possible, which made sure that they must at least be aware of our presence. The return flight was delayed for several hours and as we had not envisaged this we had used up our foreign cash and were left only with Pounds Sterling. Now that was another joke because there were no facilities to change any money within the airport and no one prepared to accept payment with British notes. Now not only did we have a screaming boy but one that was also very hungry.

When we were called to board for the journey home we had to push our way through an already crowed plane as there were people on board that had joined at Lanzarotti. Neither staff nor any one of the passengers came to our assistance, it was ignorance personified.

Of course the journey to and fro was only the start and end of the holiday, surely the bit in the middle couldn't be so bad. It has to be said that the hotel accommodation itself was lovely but those who served it and others staying there were not so grand. We managed a morning at the beach and a few sessions around the pool but as soon as Christopher started his screaming we were looked upon as something from another world. Holidaymakers in Gran Canaria are made up of a fair share of British but it seemed to us that the largest represented country was Germany. We had some Germans directly underneath our room and they seemed to get great relief from constantly ranting and raving about our little boy. One plus factor was the constant free lessons we received on German swear words; it's about all they were prepared to offer.

I do not think at any time they made the effort to find out what was the matter with Chris. In the end we could not even go to the pool without we were stared at and you knew dam well that the little congregations gathered around the perimeter were all "tittle tattling" about those Brits with the naughty little boy. Most of the time we stayed in our room, only daring to sit out on the balcony when Chris was asleep at night. Either Tina or myself would go to the restaurant and bring food back to the room so that we were able to eat without being stared at.

We did actually have one day, soon after arrival, when we decided to go to a bird and small animal sanctuary across the other side of the island. What a work up that proved to have been to walk a fair distance to the bus stop and then queue whilst Christopher decided to provide the audience with plenty of screaming. Along came the bus and we managed to squeeze on, knowing that if we waited for another it would be just as packed. Well it wasn't too bad at first but every time the bus stopped Chris started up again. How embarrassing, in a foreign country, crammed on a bus where you seem to be the only English people around and your son screeching at the top of his voice. I just do not know how we survived that bus journey but I made it very clear to Tina that no matter what the cost we would be going back by taxi.

Come to think of it, the only reason we were probably not thrown out of the hotel was because it was our own timeshare. Since returning to the UK we have never been able to contemplate another foreign holiday where we dare take Christopher with us. In fact we have not had another foreign holiday, full stop.

It has actually been very difficult to take any sort of break since that catastrophe but we have tried. We actually managed a whole three days holiday two years ago, when Chris was in respite. We were able to take little Charlie to a caravan park at Cheddar Caves, in Somerset.

This was an extremely important little break for the three of us, in particular Charlie. We were for the first time in a long while able to devote all of our time and attention to him. Let me tell you it made an enormous difference to him, his attitude and his behaviour coming on leaps and bounds. One has to say it allowed Tina and myself time to recharge our batteries, to mentally come together, a time without stress, some time for each other.

Wow! I have just realised we had a holiday last year as well. Two years on a trot, haven't we done well? Again Chris was in respite, the very last we were given, as you will find out in a later chapter. This time it was only through the generosity of one of our customers that we could afford the break. Bless them, they knew our problems and how difficult it was looking after Chris week in, week out and had picked up from our conversation that we would not be getting a holiday. To our amazement they announced that we could have the use of their caravan in Dorset for a week in the summer, at a fraction of the proper price. In fact it wasn't quite a week because the way the respite care worked it meant we had to be home in time to pick Chris up. Once again it was brilliant, this time being accompanied not only by Charlie but my oldest son Brian, his partner and their little baby girl Shanay.

It was a week again that we so badly needed, what so many take for granted was like heaven to Tina and myself. Time again to spend with Charlie without having to look over your shoulder every minute of the day. Time too, to be able to truly relax and appreciate there was a life outside of autism.

Please, let me make this very clear, that deep down we are not happy to be leaving Christopher with someone else. Indeed I can confirm that both my wife and I miss him so very much but what do you do to be right. We are told by the Paediatrician that we must spend prime time with Charlie and that we must have a break for the good of our own health. Only those reading this little book who have severely disabled children will truly appreciate both the heartache of leaving a child behind and yet the necessity of getting that all important break from time to time.

Looking at it another way, if your child is on the severe end of the spectrum, a holiday to them is not a pleasure, not something they enjoy, rather a time when they are insecure, frightened and alarmed because nothing around them is familiar.

It would seem that this year we shall not be able to indulge in a holiday, to have special time with Charlie, to recharge our overworked batteries. Having been encouraged to apply for some time where Christopher would be looked after and allow us to be like most normal families and take a holiday we applied for ten days respite, knowing and hoping that most times requests are always reduced that we might be granted seven days.

To our amazement we thought we had hit the jackpot. Yes, you can have your ten days in the summer but no nights. The offer was to take Chris on a day scheme from nine in the morning through to three in the afternoon, that's six whole hours that we would have to take a holiday.

If we chose to accept I suppose it would mean that we actually got ten holidays in one year. I am sorry to sound so sarcastic but honestly it would not be anything like six hours a day because it would be down to us to drop Chris off and to pick him up, in reality about four hours to take Charlie somewhere.

I had already found out that these ten days would be very expensive and therefore made a rational request that rather than have ten days if it would be possible to have four days and nights, thus allowing us to take a very short break away with Charlie and importantly save the local authority nearly one thousand pounds. As local governments everywhere are always bemoaning that they are cash struck we genuinely felt we were helping them as well as benefiting ourselves. Unfortunately we have been told that it is not about the money it is about our son integrating with the family more and it was suggested that I might be thinking more about my self rather than my son. If I am not mistaken I take that as an inverted way of suggesting that both my wife and I are being selfish. Are we really being selfish, when we spend so much of our time caring and loving our little boy, unable to spend prime time with Charlie, unable to relax and unwind?

It does make me wonder how much real thought goes into these decisions and what type of people make them for we never get to meet them to put our case across and one last thought on the subject, I wonder how many holidays they have each year. Having said it before so many times during conversations I reiterate my thought that unless you have a severely autistic child yourself you cannot ever hope to understand how it can affect your life. There are many great professionals in this world who serve to help look after our children but even some of the best have been the first to admit that I may be right.

I have taken advice from our local society about the negative response regarding our respite application and intend to appeal the decision and hopefully before I get to the last chapter I will be able to bring you up to date.

Chapter 14
A Shock to The System

I suppose it goes without saying that finding out Christopher was autistic and later realising just how much that would change our lives came as a real shock to both Tina and myself.

We had both experienced difficult times in our earlier years but none perhaps as difficult as those we have already negotiated since Christopher was diagnosed and without doubt those that are still ahead.

I have already spent the last chapter trying to convey what it can be like taking your autistic child on holiday, the joy and sorrow at taking a holiday without your child and the trials and tribulations one has to encounter to have your child looked after for these periods.

Having been self-employed for over twenty years it has never been a problem to think to yourself that's it, I'm having next weekend off, I'll take a few days away with the family. No boss to worry about, just please myself. Tina, too, has been self-employed now for over eight years and in the first couple of years that she had sacked her boss we were as free as the bird. Just think what a rude awakening we had when Christopher's autism really started to kick in and our lifestyles were changed forever. If you are a devoted parent and both of us consider we fall in that category there is no turning back with autism but one has to learn very quickly the best way to adjust. Tina's network marketing business, you might know it if I mention Kleeneze, led to both of us meeting new friends and an opportunity to attend conferences three times a year. Those meetings were held in Birmingham and even when Chris was young, it gave us the chance to stay over on the Saturday night and enjoy ourselves, nice food, good music and great company. My daughter would mostly oblige by staying at our house for the weekend to look after the boys but as the autism progressed her willingness to help seemed to wane. I cannot blame her for Christopher was fast becoming a real handful. It is one thing looking after a couple of normal kids but when you are faced, perhaps twice a night, with cleaning a child who has covered himself with faeces or at best spread it over the walls it is no joke.

On other occasions we had managed to get Christopher's God Mother, a qualified child care assistant, to stand in but it soon became obvious that this was all too much for her. Now these occasional weekends away were not just for pleasure, they were of course intended to teach the attendees more about the business and to mentally spur you on to do better and we felt that by going we were killing two birds with one stone, as the saying goes. What to do though when we had run out of volunteers? Well how about one of those nanny people coming in I suggested, they're qualified and whilst they won't know the children very well they should be able to cope. Every effort was made to search different agencies until one lady declared she had the perfect person for the job and she would send her over.

Well she seemed to sing the right tune so we offered her the position as occasional nanny and to make sure the boys were comfortable with her we asked her to come around a couple of times whilst we were there. Fine, as I said she seemed to know what she was talking about so we booked our conference tickets.

We left home on the Friday afternoon full of confidence in our new find and returned around two o'clock Sunday afternoon. Make no mistake we had a great weekend, pretty well relaxed knowing that at long last we would get home and not feel guilty at the horrible jobs that might have to be done, those that we did virtually every day without thinking. Pulling up outside of the house upon our return we sensed something was not quite right. Have you ever got that sort of feeling? Probably nothing to worry about, just a bit of nerves.

We were soon to find out however that our instincts were right. We entered the lounge to find that our settee had the side ripped off and later learned from our other son that Chris had repeatedly been climbing inside of it. Add that to the nest of tables he had broken and I suppose one could assume he had enjoyed himself immensely. Another really alarming thing came to the surface when we checked the freezer to find that very little of the food left for the boys and nanny had been touched. Was it ever worth going away when you consider the overall cost, our hotel for two nights about £150 plus a few bob for drinks seemed pretty insignificant when we placed it along side the cost of the nanny, two hundred pounds, cheap because we paid cash, the agency fee nearly ninety pounds and the cost of a new three piece and tables. It was not too long after this particular weekend that we gave up the two days away and any conferences we attend these days we travel to on the same day and return later that night, hoping to God that whoever has volunteered their services has come through unscathed. To be fair most of the time things don't work out too bad but they only seem to want to do it the once. To be fair we did manage to have time away at a couple more meetings when we had weekend respite for Chris but this was nipped in the bud when the respite centre was closed to overnight boarders.

Bless them, Anna and Brian my two older children, now both with families of their own will help out if we are really stuck but of course one person is not enough to look after Christopher these days, with two to one in place, we are very limited as to our chances of going anywhere together. Even an evening out for an anniversary or birthday meal is a struggle these days. If we are to venture anywhere it has to be later in the evening when Chris is settled in bed but of course even then we are on tenterhooks almost expecting the phone to ring. Where is the enjoyment in this, one might as well stay at home, have a nice steak and a bottle of bubbly and most of all not have the worry.

More than one person has asked us why we bother working, knowing that we do more hours on duty at home than many work in a full time job. "Let Mr Blair keep you," one suggested, but we are not that type of people. We are definitely not parasites. We want to feel we are doing our bit and in any case running our little business not only gives us a feeling of partial independence but also helps us retain our sanity. We work jolly hard whilst the boys are at school and make sure we have plenty of banter between ourselves and with our customers. It is amazing how many of our customers, being aware of our circumstances, take a real interest in the boys welfare, it is many of the same people that have urged me on to put pen to paper and write this book.

There are those who tell us they regularly pray for our family, those that bring Tina flowers from the church and those who so genuinely offer words of comfort. To all of those wonderful people I am going to use this opportunity to say a special thank you and God bless you for your caring ways and messages of support.

Thank goodness the people on the other side of the fence are in the minority but we have had it inferred that we have used our sons as an excuse why we have not done more with our lives and our business. To those poor souls I feel sympathy and can only assume that they have made their judgement without first fully understanding the true reality of having to live life engulfed in a never-ending sea of torrent. Perhaps it may also be a case best summed up so aptly by the old saying, "I'm alright Jack," for as much as some do not care about others they still think they have the right to criticise. There is an old Latin saying which I shall not even attempt to spell, albeit that I can say it but in English it translates to "Evil unto him who evil thinks." With that let us move on.

This living with autism has not only been a shock to our systems but a real shock to our pockets. When in 2004 we took the bold decision to call time on the driving school it was done without too much thought about the financial implications, the most important reason being the need for both Tina and myself needing to care for Chris as he became more difficult and provide extra time to spend with Charlie. It would have been all too easy to find ourselves regretting that decision, to be forever moaning about how tight things were but what is the point? Whilst it is nice to have financial independence surely it is far more important under our circumstances to have time available to give one hundred per cent effort to the boys. As I have already said we love to work, I used to do fifty to sixty lessons a week one time, Tina worked long hard hours but now we have our priorities right. If we cannot afford something today there is always tomorrow and if money could be converted to love we have an abundance within our four walls.

Yes, it was hard at the start, there are times when we still have a tear or two, but doesn't everyone have to conquer an "Everest" somewhere throughout their lives?

We are still climbing, not even half way up our mountain but one thing is for sure, there is no turning back. We are focussed on reaching the top, to keep our lives on track but not forgetting that unless a miracle cure is uncovered we will never return to life as it was before. I expect Christopher ruled by his autism will have many more shocks in store for us but hell, we have to take whatever he gives, get back up and fight on.

Chapter 15
Living On Egg Shells

Relax, take it easy, are words we have had directed towards us so many times and I wish it was that simple. No matter where you are, in the car, visiting a relative, at the doctors or at hospital there is absolutely no way that you can relax. You certainly cannot even do that at home, let alone when you are out some place.

Fear takes the place of relaxation in our lives, never knowing whether we have Mr Jeckel or Mr Hyde to look after. I suppose its not so bad if we are at home for at least then if Christopher decides to break something, spill his or someone else's drink quite deliberately or even physically attack somebody it is contained within our four walls. I am not saying it has less effect on you it definitely does not, but at least you are saved the embarrassment of having to apologise for your son's behaviour. You cannot sit in your own home and chill out, you are up and down following Chris around to make sure you can scupper his next plan. Little Charlie might be sat on the sofa, minding his own business, watching the box and for no reason whatsoever Chris will attack him, sometimes slapping between the shoulder blades, other times pulling his hair or perhaps just giving him a real hard pinch.

On other occasions it might be his mum that he picks on and most times not for any specific reason. However just two or three weeks ago Tina was out in the garden with Christopher and he was enjoying bouncing up and down on the trampoline when suddenly he jumped off and ran into the rabbit shed. Very unusual for him to do so as he normally runs a mile from any animal so Tina went over to keep an eye on him. He was alright for a while, just looking in the hutches but then he started to pick up the droppings from the shed floor and flatly refused to stop when told by his mum. Thinking of the hygiene Tina tried to get him out of the shed and this was like waving a red rag to a bull. He turned and attacked her with all of his might; pinching her in some very painful places, he was totally uncontrollable. For a comparatively little boy he is so strong, so determined, never taking in to account that you might be twice his size. I was actually up stairs in the office checking the latest emails and although being quite deaf could hear the commotion going on outside. It is not easy for me to hurry, just recovering from both shoulder and knee operations in the last six months but I made it in time to see Christopher still turning on his mum. To be honest it was all we could do between us to get him into the house and to the safety of his padded room where we let his tantrum run its course, knowing that whilst he was in his bedroom the chances of him hurting himself were greatly reduced.

Chris gets a great kick out of doing anything that will get a reaction. People have questioned how intelligent he really is, I tell you he is one clever little fella. A good example would be when he sneaks into the kitchen and maybe grabs a bottle of milk that you have mistakenly left out, pours it all over the floor and then repeats time and time again, "don't pour the milk over," or words to that effect. Try telling me he does not know what he is doing. What's more how many of you out there could just accept this and say nothing, bearing in mind that this is not a one off, he is always looking for his next trick. Perhaps one of the most annoying is when you have poured yourself some fruit juice and you get distracted leaving your glass on the table and on your return you find it filled up with pieces of paper or even more disgusting objects.

I have already told you how we are on edge when we visit my sister but it is the same wherever we go. Mind, my brother in law says he loves Chris and I am sure he does but I think that relationship was stretched to its limits when Christopher decided to pull pieces of the wallpaper off just days after it had been repainted. He is so crafty with it and lures you somehow into a false sense of security, you thinking he's sat nicely for once and then you find out what his hidden hand has been up to. You know my brother in law looks like old Ronnie Barker and sometimes sounds like him when he spots Chris up to something, you know the "De De De De De What's he Doing?" Of course I'll do my best to intervene but at the same time I have to have a chuckle, you know what they say, "If you don't laugh sometimes you'd cry."

Without exaggeration the whole of every day, whilst Christopher is awake, whether we are at home, in the car or out somewhere for a while, is a test of our nerves and our patience. I am sure it is exactly the same for his teachers; even with all of their experience they cannot predict when or where he will strike next. Even the most necessary of appointments, maybe the doctors or paediatrician, can prove to be unbearable. It is the unpredictability that sets you on edge, wondering what's going through your son's mind; it just wears you down some days.

One visit to see the paediatrician sticks in my mind when Chris virtually wrecked the room whilst we were trying to concentrate with the doctor. We were up and down from our chairs, trying to prevent him tearing things off the walls, stop him turning the taps on full, trash the cupboards and throw the toys he had been offered all over the place. I suppose it did us one big favour in that the doctor was able to see him at his worst; she didn't need to just accept our word. What caused him to go off on one that day? Well we believe it was simply the fact that we tried to get him to stand still on the scales for his weight and height.

Let's just tell you about some more problems that have occurred in our home, as if it is not enough when you have someone visit to be on tenterhooks, hoping Chris will behave you have to put up with the embarrassment when he decides to perform. We had some friends in one day, colleagues in the business, and we were all enjoying a cuppa and catching up on the gossip when our little angel decided to mess himself, put his hands down his trousers and run around the room smearing over anything and everything in sight. Is it really any wonder that people who want to come and see us ask if they can come during the day whilst both boys are at school? I mean, what must it feel like to people coming in doors, to experience something like that incident, they come to see us for what is assumed will be a pleasant time and have to witness such an awful scene. All we can do is apologise and hope that they will stay whilst we set about cleaning up Chris and the room.

On more than one occasion he has chosen his moment to pull down the top of his trousers and wee over the carpet or an armchair, without any consideration who we might have visiting. When he intends to do this he makes sure he has your attention by repeatedly shouting, "Needy the toilet," then as soon as you turn round he will start his performance knowing that you are far enough away not to be able to do anything about it, save go red down to the waist line and then escort him off to the toilet.

There have been occasions when we have braved having some of the family round, or maybe friends for dinner but we are extremely apprehensive every time. What can be worse, when your beautiful little boy, sitting at one end of the table, launches a missile, it could be some food he has already chewed, aiming it at someone at the other end. He may also dump some of his food on to your plate but surely you must agree that the worst possible thing is when he waits to ensure you are distracted, leans forward, and spits on your dinner. I maybe could somehow find a way of still eating my food but it is again the sheer embarrassment. You sort of know what your company might be thinking, "what are they doing allowing him to do that, haven't they trained him with better manners?"

Christopher has a brilliant throwing arm as I have already said and whenever he goes into the garden we start to worry. Our next door neighbours have recently had a lovely double glazed sun lounge built on the back of their property and at about the same time Chris has decided he wants to throw his toys and stones if available over the fence, some of it hitting the windows and some landing on the roof of the sun lounge. The neighbours are fairly understanding but you know what's coming when you see them approaching your front door with a carrier bag in their hand. We are presented with the bag and it's contents and asked in as many words to try and prevent a recurrence. That's easier said than done because it takes just seconds for him to grab something and provide an encore. To stop him completely means either locking our back door and not letting him out to the garden or to erect what could be an unsightly high fence although I am not sure the latter would work as he has learnt to clear a twelve foot fence with objects at school. Talking about locking the back door, we had trouble doing that for a few days, the key was missing. Guess where it was spotted? It was on the roof of the neighbours sun lounge. You just cannot win.

Something that really concerns us is when Anna or Brian visit and Christopher targets one of their children, two of which are only babies. No matter how cautious you may be, trying to always ensure that at least one adult remains in the room on the alert, there is always going to be the times when for some reason the plan falls through. It may only be for seconds but that is all Christopher needs to slap one of the little ones. He is even brazen enough to attack when you are still in the room, sometimes only inches away from his target. He just gradually moves closer to you, again leading you into that false sense of security, then slapping, launches the assault, followed by the by now customary smile. Mission accomplished for Chris but once again we are left feeling deflated, defeated and not knowing quite what to say.

When you sit back and think this problem through I suppose neither Tina or myself must blame ourselves but in these situations you do not think straight away that your child is autistic, that he has problems, you only think that is my child and he has misbehaved and I am totally responsible just as you would if your son or daughter was normal. This is something, no matter how many people try to convince us otherwise that will I guess continue with Chris not able to accept what he has done is wrong and Tina and I as parents picking up the guilt.

Chapter 16
Taking Stock

I thought at this time it might be good to think back and tell you about some of the trophies Christopher has collected so far on his journey with severe autism. It is not just the value of things he has broken, nor the sentimental side but perhaps more importantly the danger to him self and others.

It is important too to realise that whilst some things are as a result of sudden impulse or perhaps brought on by a tantrum that others can be a carefully planned operation. Tina has always had a love for owls and has collected ornaments of various sizes throughout her life and when I found out that one of our customers actually made porcelain ornaments and I saw how beautiful they were I put in my order. I decided to go for an owl that stood some fifteen inches tall and when completed and painted it looked really impressive, I knew Tina would love it.

"Be careful," I said, "It's very fragile," as she unpacked the present. She was absolutely amazed at the splendour but immediately her thoughts went on to where we were going to keep it safe. In the corner of our sun lounge we have three shelves one of which is at least six feet high, we would place the owl on this, where it would be perfectly safe. We noticed over the next three or four weeks Chris was quite often looking upwards at the new arrival but we were confident that it was safe from his grasp. Next to the shelves was a computer table on which was a computer tower and monitor, which had been given to us for use by the boys. It was old and ran on Windows ninety-five but good enough for Charlie to play some games on, keeping him off of the computer we used for business. Next to the computer stood a solid rocking horse, again a gift for the boys from a neighbour whose children and grandchildren had grown out of but it was ideal for Christopher in particular and not just for its designed purpose.

We were having a cup of tea with some of our team members when Christopher arrived home on the school bus and both Tina and myself, as always, went out to escort him into the house. Once he made it inside he ran for the back of the house, nothing unusual, as we had started to encourage him to at least sit on the toilet when he got home. This afternoon was different however, running straight past the bathroom into the sun lounge where he started his mountaineering. Obviously, what Chris had seen and been working out for a while was not so obvious to us but he wasted no time in climbing on the rocking horse, up on to the computer table and finally on to the computer monitor and it was from this precarious position that he was able to reach the prized owl and send it tumbling to the floor. "Oh poor Owl," was his reaction to the dozens of pieces strewn across the floor. It was the speed of his operation that caught us out, all over in seconds; our plans to keep the ornament safe were scuppered. Our friends just look on in amazement and like us disbelief that someone not only with severe autism but also so young could be ingenious enough to work something out this clever. I offered to have a replacement made but Tina made the point that no matter where it was placed it would never be safe and what's more that she would be constantly worrying about it.

Now, I mentioned a computer and a monitor both fairly heavy objects that were in the sun lounge for Charlie to use at his leisure. It was soon to become a thing of the past because Christopher decided during a massive tantrum to drag the monitor onto the floor and break it, mission accomplished as far as he was concerned.

So that was the Owl and the "Puter" as Chris says it, both sent to the scrap yard, but it wasn't the last thing in the sun lunge that he targeted. A few months later a fourteen-inch television was donated to the boys, replacing the entertainment Charlie had got from the computer. However Chris was not prepared to leave it sitting nicely on a shelf; when he had yet another tantrum. Just as we thought he had calmed down he made a dash for the Television and literally threw it across the room ensuring that it was impossible to use in the future.

Shall we move into another room now? Just in case you think that the sun lounge was the only one to encounter Christopher's wrath. Well in the kitchen, he has broken off several of the doors on the kitchen units, they are held in place thanks to a very good filler and that stuff "No more nails." Then there's the microwave door. For this manoeuvre he enlisted the help of the washing up bowl, turning it upside down to use as a step and then by head butting smashed the glass door. Once again you might ask, "Where's his parents," but I assure you he is clever enough and quick enough to wait his chance when your back is turned, maybe you have only popped to the loo or been distracted by someone else, it takes him just seconds to do something like that. Other items that have copped it in the kitchen are glasses, plates, cups, and all manner of things that give him pleasure in smashing.

I think one of his favourites was milk bottles, preferably full ones, whether they were left out on top or in the fridge, he would target them first pouring out any milk and then slamming them on the floor. He would do just the same if he saw the bottles near the front door and for this reason we chose to cancel our milk delivery. You know how you feel perhaps when someone like your wife breaks your favourite mug or dinner plate, utterly deflated, you don't want to moan because you know it was a complete accident but deep down you're heartbroken, you think to yourself, "I've had that for years," now gone forever. That's a bit like it feels when Christopher breaks or destroys things, you know he can't really help it but he's going to keep doing it anyway, only just sometimes I do wonder if he has some idea that he knows that something just happens to be your pride and joy. I suppose we will never know what goes on inside that little head of his. Oh, just before we leave the kitchen let's not forget the glass in the window that he head butted and broke, amazingly not cutting himself in the process.

Remember I told you about the settee he tore when the Nanny looked after him and Charlie, well that's only the start in the lounge. There have been several small tables he has broken, chewed the wooden back of one of our dining room chairs, part of a dining room suite that we were really proud of and bitten holes in a couple of the cushions. Ornaments have totally disappeared from view partly because he has broken so many and the remainder hidden away for their own safety. Then there's the carpet and the underlay. Chris loves to get behind the sofa and if you're not watching he will pull up the carpet and tear pieces of the underlay up and make sure you know he has done it. "Oh Poor Carpet," he recites.

Obviously with the settee damaged beyond repair we had to find a replacement and we had the opportunity to buy a lovely little leather three-piece suite from one of my daughters friends, not new but in good order and it suited our budget. Another bonus would be being able to wipe it clean easily should Chris have one of his wetting sessions. We were so pleased when it arrived, something in our home once again that looked relatively new, boy were we lucky? Well I suppose we were in a way for it lasted a whole week before Christopher decided in one of his tantrums to bite a hole in the settee. Fortunately there was just about enough slack to tuck the leather over and stick it down with super glue. Well that sorted things for the time being but within another few weeks when he flipped again, he bit a hole in an armchair so again out came the super glue, not so easy this time but we managed a botched job. Whether Christopher didn't like that suite I will never know but through his determined efforts to charge at the settee, throwing himself on it, he broke the support at the back and so once again we were on the look out for a replacement.

We did have a border around the room about half way up the wall but Chris saw this off just a few weeks after we had decorated meaning the whole room had to be repainted. In fact any room, which had a border, has now had to be repainted minus the added decoration. One of his other tricks is to bang the walls with toys or plastic plates making sure that dents appear all over the place.

Let's step outside for a moment and tell you about the really cool gnome we bought to brighten things up in the back garden. It stood about three feet tall, well for just over four hours anyway, until Christopher picked it up and threw it over the back wall breaking it to bits. Guess what he said? You've got it, "Oh Poor Hi Ho." To us it was nineteen pounds ninety-nine pence down the drain and a good lesson learnt.

Many of Christopher's other destructive habits take place any where he fancies, any where he spots an opportunity, like watching when you have put your spectacles down somewhere, waiting for you to look away at which point he will grab them. You are very lucky indeed if you retrieve them in one piece. It got so bad, much through my own carelessness because I don't always stop and think when I take my glasses off, that I began buying cheaper pairs of reading glasses for example when we went to Cheddar I bought three pairs in the Pound Shop. What's the point of spending out loads more when they are quite suitable for my son to break?

Books, newspapers, the post and Charlie's homework assignments are often shredded behind our backs and sometimes quite blatantly in front of us once Chris has worked out he is just far enough away so that we cannot prevent him from having a ripping time. Soft toys do not stand a chance with Christopher. We cannot give him any in his own room, they would be torn to shreds in minutes but what he will do is run into his brother's room, pinch a cuddly and again before we can react he has it in pieces. Sometimes this has been so difficult for little Charlie for it has been some of his old favourites that have bitten the dust. Christopher loves it because whilst Tina and I have learnt, well at least some of the time, not to react Charlie always does; he falls right into the trap.

Before the days of the padded bedroom Chris would do his best to wreck any furniture he had including the bed itself. Even since the transformation of his room he has found much to take apart. Where he gets the strength from is a mystery but he has pulled some of the padded squares off the wall and pulled up some of the ones on the floor, all of which had been securely screwed in place. The waterproof mattress he has is very heavy and jammed in position but that has not stopped our little boy, if he takes it in his head to move it so be it. One of the most frustrating things he does is to repeatedly tear up his bedclothes. We started by giving him a duvet with a character cover but after he had torn several of these up we decided to raid the loft and use any blankets that we still had. After a while we had exhausted the supply of blankets, most having been torn into strips no wider than an inch or two and so now we have reverted to the duvet, buying three or four at a time of the Tesco value range. Believe it or not during the cold nights when you would think he would want to keep wrapped up he went through six duvets in one week. If they are not torn up they are so badly stained by his faeces that the bin is the only logical place for them to end up. We have exactly the same problem with pillows, to the point where we have temporarily given up giving him one in the hope that he may realise he is missing out on something.

Special sleep suits costing around twenty pounds each, bought to prevent him access to his nappy, proved to be useless. He just tore them up like paper as nothing was going to prevent him getting to his artistic materials. So now we just use ordinary pyjamas, some times they still get torn up but more often than not he just strips them off thank goodness. This habit of tearing clothes does not stop in his bedroom, no matter what time of day, where he is or who is looking after him if he decides to tear something up there is little you can do to stop him, once again it is his timing and speed of delivery. At his first school as you will hear later, we had bags of clothes sent home that he had ripped to pieces, not necessarily the school's fault but very frustrating and costly for us having to replace them at such regularity.

Neither my wife or myself are too proud to admit that we have found many of the answers on Ebay, buying up job lots at very reasonable prices, knowing that they probably were not going to last long anyway. Purchasing clothes like this has helped stay within our family budget and meant that we have been able to keep both boys reasonably clothed. If you are personally affected in a similar way to us do remember that there are plenty of bargains, many including brand names, that you can buy for much less than it would cost in the shops and after all who knows where you have bought them from?

To finish off this chapter I would just like to tell you a little about the damage to our poor old car. Remember earlier in the book I mentioned we had been given protective shields and that Christopher had broken these with his bare feet. Well that's not all. Very shortly after buying the vehicle on the mobility scheme he broke the air conditioning vents behind the front seats whilst other damage includes holes bitten in the head rests, kicking various pieces of trim out of line and pulling the overhead light out of its fixing, to name but a few. You know when we bought this car we were given two options, one, have a brand new car which would be taxed and serviced for us for three years after which we could change it in for another or the option which we chose to buy a second hand car using the mobility money but tax, insure and service it ourselves.

Boy am I glad we made the right choice for if we had gone for a new vehicle we would have been expected to keep it in pristine condition and have stuck to a restricted mileage each year. Just think what condition the new car would have finished up in, I mean do you really think it would have made a difference to Chris?

There are so many more instances of damage I could relate to, probably enough to add another couple of pages to this chapter but I hope by now I have given you a flavour, an idea of just how bad things can get. Please don't leave this part of the book thinking that everything that Christopher does is destructive, it would be totally wrong. There are many loving memories of our sweet little boy who just seconds after he has broken your heart will mend it in the time it takes to click your fingers.

Chapter 17
The Face Of An Angel

I mentioned in the last chapter that Chris is not always up to no good, sometimes, not too often, he takes you by complete surprise especially now his vocabulary is improving. With his beautiful little angelic face he will come right up to you, only inches from your own face and say "Hello Mummy" or "Hello Daddy," I tell you it means so very much to us.

There are times when totally out of the blue he will walk up to you and say "Kiss Mummy" or "Kiss Daddy," things that are probably taken for granted by so many become treasures for us as parents. Christopher has also got into giving spontaneous cuddles, not just to Tina and myself but also to his brothers, sister, his nieces and nephew. Sounds funny doesn't it, eight years old and he has four nieces and one nephew, all of which he has given a slap or two so we still have to keep a very good eye on him. The trouble is you don't know when he gets near one of the children which it is going to be, a smack or a cuddle but you try to hold back from the situation a little hoping that this time it is going to be the latter. If you're not prepared to give him at least some trust he is never going to move on and we are denying him a chance to show his nice side.

How wonderful was it for us to hear him recently count up to four? How marvellous, when at his fourth birthday party he blew his candles out, all on his own, for the first time. I mean surely this is something we all take for granted with ordinary children but a moment to truly savour when it's your autistic son. Another first, last Christmas being the first year he has opened all of his presents without our help. Important too that instead of just tearing into them that he took his time and studied each one a little before moving on to the next.

Two years ago we bought Charlie a twelve foot trampoline for his birthday but his brother would go no where near it, in facts attempts to put him on there have resulted in major tantrums and screaming. How cool, when last November the fifth, on my birthday, which just happens to be Guy Fawlkes night and all the family were round to enjoy a few fireworks and a glass of bubbly, Christopher completed a double. He not only watched the display without too much fuss but also watched it whilst bouncing up and down on the trampoline. I bet you've guessed, we now have a tough job getting him off of there sometimes.

Whilst most of his speech is still echolalic it is wonderful to hear him sometimes ask for what he wants, albeit very simply but to listen to that sweet little boy say "Drink please" or just "Want Tigers," that's cornflakes to Chris, is so satisfying and leaves Tina and myself on a real high.

This chapter is not too long but I cannot leave it without first telling you what has happened whilst I have been writing these very words. Christopher, as if he knew which chapter I was working on, came into the office just a few moments ago, sat down beside me, probably wondering what I was up to and said, "Hello Dad." Perhaps when I tell you that with his next breath he said, "Love you Daddy," you will understand why I am sat here covered in Goose Bumps. That I will treasure forever, the most magical moment of my life. I pray now that he will choose an equally well-chosen time to say similar to his mum, God bless him!

Chapter 18
Like A Day At The Races

Taking Christopher to hospital is very much like going for a day out at the races. Why? Well it is all a gamble as to whether you come out feeling up or down and this depends on so many factors, none of which we have any real control over. Unlike the racehorse that may fall at a fence or hurdle and not carry on we have learnt the only way is to pick ourselves up and get on with it.

Firstly, let's look at the factors that rely on Christopher himself, where perhaps we can at least have a little influence. It all depends on his mood on the day, how he feels generally and whether or not he is prepared to accept whatever distraction we have put in place, such as a favourite toy, the occasional sweetie or his present and perhaps all time favourite, stickers. Stickers are something that he loves, painstakingly taking them from the sheet and placing them on his piece of card. He will spend hours on this activity, the only problem being that during this craze he uses not just a few but hundreds of "Stickys," as he calls them. Not that we mind when he is at hospital, if it calms him its money well spent.

The difference between Christopher's hospital visits running smoothly or being quite disastrous can also without doubt depend on how long we are kept waiting and the attitude and understanding of the nursing staff. It has to be said that most of the doctors who have seen Christopher have been prepared to listen to us and take on board how we feel it best to deal with any given situation.

Any hospital for any child is a very daunting experience, not knowing perhaps where they are going, why they are attending but for an autistic child those problems can be ten times worse. Before the days of the buggy when Chris had to go in hospital for a blood test it was a truly exhausting and frightening experience. I remember it well, he would not walk in so it was a case of carrying him all the way from the car park to the butterfly room and as if that wasn't enough having to wrestle with him to keep him still while the magic cream was applied and eventually the blood was taken. He has had to have several blood tests over his brief few years so far and thankfully now having a buggy and by liasing with the team in the butterfly room things have got a little easier. We ring up to say we are due in and on arrival let the staff know where we are and the magic cream is applied straight away and we are back out of the hospital building, away from the crowds, within minutes, only returning when his hands and arms are anaesthetised sufficiently. Once back at the butterfly room Christopher is fitted in to the next slot and we are on our way. I think one person deserves special mention in the quest for Christopher's blood. It was on the very first time we went for this purpose, as I said no buggy and Chris was really on form, fighting and screaming all the way through. Then came a guy named Rob, a play nurse in the section who asked what Chris was into at that time. When we told him he liked string Rob was off to find some but came back empty handed. Wait a minute, Chris had spotted that Rob, our saviour for the day, had lace up shoes. Without any hesitation Rob removed his laces and allowed Chris to play with them, a job well done but one hell of a game getting the laces back to their rightful owner.

During a period late in 2004 when Christopher's behaviour appeared to be getting worse by the day the paediatrician suggested we change his medication, at least for a while, to see if it would make any significant difference. He had been on Ritalin and this was changed to Strattera, all we could do was wait to see the effects. Well to be honest it did not take long at all because apart from not improving Chris's behavioural pattern it also seemed influential in him becoming ill. He became very lethargic, ate nothing and barely drank anything for five days. After taking advice from the family doctor and paediatrician it was decided that we take Christopher straight to the Child assessment unit at the hospital where the first task was to try and get fluids into him. It was decided not to do this intravenously because he was so agitated and constantly thrashing out. Instead fluids were to be given orally as often as possible using a syringe, which was fine, but during this period we saw little of any nurses and the enforced drinking was left for us to do.

It was actually very amusing, no hilarious is the word, when having been given a jelly to try and encourage him to eat, Christopher decided to throw it at the consultant who had come in to examine him. This gentleman had visited Chris earlier and had said that he was admitting him but it wasn't long after the green wobbly mass had stained his suit that he returned with an alternative suggestion. "Yes, I want to admit your son but because of his explosive nature it would be best if you took him home at night and brought him back by seven thirty each morning. He will be treated as an in patient but we have not got the staff or facilities to look after him in here." So there it was, for the remainder of Christopher's stay in hospital, which was three days, we had to remain on the ward until about nine each evening, take him home and be back early the next morning. The second morning we arrived there was no bed for him and we were asked to wait in a side room. In here we noticed blood over the floor and someone had left a "Sharps Container" within easy reach and you can probably guess what Christopher did next. He pulled free from my grasp picked up the container and threw it across the room, spilling all sorts of syringes and blood stained objects across the floor. I grabbed Chris up in my arms, carried him out and flatly refused to re-enter that room. Whether it was our actions that caused a delay I am not sure but we were left waiting around for what seemed like an eternity. Surely we asked, shouldn't a hospital as big as this one have a safe room, should we really have been sent home, when our son clearly wasn't well enough to do so and what if we lived much further away, what if our son suddenly became worse? I must add that until we made a bit of a fuss that there was very little effort to provide backup whilst we took turns in taking refreshments ourselves. Fortunately Chris recovered and it was decided to change his medication back to Ritalin.

It wasn't too long after this episode that we found ourselves back in the hospital. Christopher had looked very ill when we went to get him up and by coincidence we were due that day to see his community paediatrician, a smashing lady, understanding and caring. She did not hesitate and gave us a letter to take to the hospital; to the same unit we had been in before. Before we left she rang a senior doctor requesting that she see us upon arrival.

What a game we had, sitting waiting for several hours, having junior doctors looking at Christopher and flatly refusing to inform their senior we had arrived. It wasn't until we threatened to walk out and go elsewhere and made a call back to our local paediatrician that we got any action.

In fact Tina had gone to the car for a break when the senior turned up. I told her how cross we were that no one had listened and I was very surprised when she personally offered to entertain Chris whilst I took the lift downstairs to fetch Tina. What a difference between people, this lady was so understanding, prepared to listen to us and take on board our thoughts. She personally took blood tests and said she would see us as soon as they were back and true to her word she did so. Nothing particularly showed up however so she decided to supply us with a blood-monitoring machine so that whenever Chris had a turn we could test his blood and pass on the results to the hospital. I suppose the point I am trying to make is that some people do not really seem to take into account that without any additional illness you still have a very difficult child to look after whilst others tackle your situation in a far more caring manner.

It was decided not long afterwards to run some more tests on Christopher, the view being that he may possibly be diabetic. There was one particular morning when Christopher was fine when he left home but within an hour we were called by the school to say that he was extremely pale and lifeless, we set off immediately armed with the monitor. On arrival we immediately tested his blood to find the reading was more than three times higher than normal. Just in case this was a mistake we repeated the test after fifteen minutes receiving a very similar result. Deciding there was something clearly wrong we rang the hospital and we were told to take him in as soon as possible. Now this time how different things were with a senior doctor on hand to receive us and yet another coming along within minutes. There were a whole number of additional tests conducted that day and it was suggested as Christopher's sugar levels had dropped back down that it would be in his best interest to be at home, whilst we awaited the results. We were not to worry; if anything came back that needed treating urgently they would contact us. It was so different from our previous visit.

In November 2005 Tina and I had been invited by our group leader to a Christmas party but it meant that we would have to stay overnight in Gloucester. As luck would have it Chris was in respite this weekend so we were free to attend. We were having a cracking time when one of the cares at the home rang to say she suspected that Christopher had Scarlet Fever and would we give permission for a doctor to see him. God were we worried; of course we gave our permission and offered to try to get back that night. Having been assured he was alright we decided to stay and leave early the next morning, a good thing really for I am not sure how we would have got home, bearing in mind we had both had a couple of drinks.

Why do I include this episode in a chapter where I am writing about his time at hospital? Well, one of the after affects of the scarlet fever was to leave him with very bad squints in both eyes.

We went through the normal channels and were referred to the Eye Unit with a request that Chris be seen as soon as possible because the squints were very bad indeed. Sometimes so bad that you could not see much of the eye at all. I must say things moved pretty quickly and we soon found ourselves sat in the waiting room of the local Eye Hospital. They were brilliant, making sure that Christopher was not kept waiting any longer than necessary and that all of the tests were conducted using machinery that caused him less stress.

After a second visit it was decided to supply Chris with a specially prepared bendy pair of spectacles in the hope that regular use just might help the problem. Have you ever tried getting your child to put sun glasses on, I mean how long do they stay there once in position. Picture us trying to get Christopher to wear his glasses. It took a great deal of patience, there were some days when we were lucky, others when he flatly refused to co-operate. I think the coup de grace was one hour whilst he watched television and was bribed with a packet of crisps but mostly we were lucky to achieve five minutes maximum.

It became clear that the spectacles were not going to have the desired effect and so it was decided that surgery was the only answer. The great thing about this was that the surgeon realised how difficult it was going to be, made sure that Christopher would be seen very soon and that on the big day he would be near the beginning of the list. It is a strange situation when you take your child in for day surgery on their eyes. Firstly there is no proper designated place to get them changed, we used the corner of the waiting room and secondly after surgery they do not return to the eye unit but upstairs on a children's ward. We were permitted to take Chris to theatre and Tina went with our little fella into the anaesthetic room, staying with him until he was safely asleep.

The next hour and a half seemed like an eternity, when would they call us to accompany Chris to the ward. Eventually a nurse showed us the way to the recovery unit and one did not have any trouble in identifying which cubicle Christopher was in. The poor little chap was thrashing out, screaming and totally inconsolable but the specialist looking after him was lovely both to us and to our son, a true professional. After about half an hour we were ready to roll, to move Chris up to the ward and this is where everything changed.

We were accompanied by a nurse from the children's ward and on the way there Chris was lashing out trying everything he could to get off the trolley, with only Tina and myself seemingly doing anything to prevent him. You may find it hard to believe what happened next for as we arrived at the ward Christopher pulled out the drip needle from his arm and put it in his mouth. Alarmed, I shouted to the nurse that had travelled with us and told her the problem, only to be told to remove the needle. Now was that my job, was not our son in hospital care and why did my wife have to apply pressure on Chris's arm to prevent blood spurting out? I was fuming, so cross at the attitude. Christopher was bandaged up and it was again up to us to keep him on the bed but as things got more difficult, with Chris screaming the place down, I looked across the ward to see five nurses just stood at their station, were none of them going to make a move to help? Truth is no, not until I shouted across and made it clear we needed assistance.

One answer we were given to the problem, just forty-five minutes after Christopher had come back from theatre, was to take him home. How could we manage that, how could that be safe when he was still thrashing out and was clearly not with it? Thank the Lord one nurse on the ward took up the challenge and offered us help. She was so kind, getting Christopher drink and later something to eat after which he seemed to calm down. That day proved so difficult for us all and to this day we cannot begin to understand what pain Christopher must have been in and what was running through his mind.

Thankfully since that awful day in our lives we have returned to the Eye unit for Christopher to be given the all clear, his eyes are now perfect and following an eye test using very small pictures we are informed that he has fighter pilot quality vision. Look out in a few years.

Since Chris has been at Hope Lodge School, something you will hear more about a little later, it has been almost a delight to go to the hospital. On one of the Eye check ups and when he required some more blood tests and x-rays two of his teachers have come with us, armed with all sorts of distractions and I must say singing voices to die for. Seriously what a help they have been. Let me tell you and I am sure this will raise a chuckle when we had the latest lot of x-rays taken. We arrived in good time and the hospital staff was thankfully waiting for us and Christopher at that point seemed fairly calm. Well that is until we tried to put him up on the table for the x-ray. Picture it, three of us fitted out with lead suits, my wife and a teacher trying to hold Christopher's feet still and myself at his top end trying to do similar. It finished up with myself virtually lying across him, my feet off the ground pushing against a cupboard behind me for added power and the ladies lying across his feet. It must have been so hilarious for the radiographer but she was really over the moon to get so much help with such a difficult patient.

Hopefully, other than treatment for his autism, Christopher will steer clear of hospitals for years to come and I just hope by including these experiences they will be both of interest and bring awareness to some of the problems parents with autistic children have to face. One thing is for sure, always remember you want what is best for your child, don't be afraid to speak out, be prepared to jump any hurdle that you come across. We have found that if you are prepared to do this, make the doctors well aware that your child does not take well to waiting that most of them will cooperate. I say this not to knock the medical profession but some doctors that are expert in their own fields do not understand the totally different world of autism and to prove my point let me just leave this chapter by asking a question to those of you who have children with severe autism. If you have taken your child to hospital with a problem not necessarily related to autism how many doctors start asking your child questions? How are you today, where does it hurt and so on? I know it has happened to us.

Chapter 19
The Memory Man

Not being a medical expert I do not know the answer to the following question. Does having an exceedingly good memory mean you are intelligent? If it does then we may have proof of what Tina and myself have suspected all along, that Christopher, although severely autistic, is reasonably clever. It has been a subject debated since Christopher was first diagnosed as to whether the autism was in fact clouding his intelligence.

Some of the things he has said and done over the last few years have been incredible, like the time I wondered why I couldn't get any television channels and then realised the sky card was missing. As you do, perhaps talking almost to yourself, I happened to say, "Christopher have you taken the card out of this machine." To my amazement he trotted off to the kitchen, opened the cupboard door under the sink and pointed to a vase. Sure enough down at the bottom of the vase, which incidentally was not see through so we wouldn't have noticed anything in it, there was the missing card. Fantastic but we still couldn't put the telly on because it had been well and truly chewed. The two things however that amazed us were firstly that he understood what I had said in the first place and secondly that he had remembered exactly what he had done with the card. It was perhaps the first positive indication that our son understood more than we had previously given him credit for.

It is only fairly recently that Christopher decided he liked chips, not the ones cooked at home and they had to be in a cone. We have from time to time as a treat given Chris and Charlie McDonalds both always having a chicken nugget meal. All that Chris would eat was the nuggets, leaving an extra portion of fries for his brother or mummy and daddy might share them but now we lose out Christopher eats the lot. He has gone "chip" mad, constantly requesting them when we are out in the car, whether it be early morning on the way to school or some other time when chip shops are shut.

What is amazing however is his memory as to where the McDonalds shops are in our area together with knowing all of the fish and chip shops through out the town. Please do not go thinking we go to all of them but in the course of delivering our orders each week we do pass quite a number. The boys are with us some times if we have a few orders still outstanding when they get home from school and Christopher wastes no time at all ranting and raving about "Chippies." I have even tried taking diversions from the normal routes but he always seems to know. I think one of the funniest things happened just a few days ago, when we were out working and Christopher was with us as it was half term. It was around about lunch time and rather than go all the way home for a snack Tina and I decided to be naughty and have a chip buttie and of course I got the cone of chips for Christopher. Rather than just take them from me and get tucked in he complained profusely in his own way that I hadn't got a sausage to go with the chips. There we were parked in a lay by on a main road hoping to enjoy what was a rare treat for us, whilst Chris repeatedly shouted at the top of his voice "Not got sausage, not got sausage."

It's not much better with ice-cream vans, he knows there is one generally parked on the sea front so if I turn off before getting to it he goes mad, God knows what other people think, for he must be heard for miles.

Chris is also extremely good with remembering names, even people he may only have met one or two times. He surprised my neighbour recently by saying her new born son's name to her when she was out in the garden, "Where's Ben," he shouted from the trampoline. I know it might not seem too much to some for an eight year old to remember the names of his family, including the babies whose names are rather unusual, Shanay and Shanai but to us it is truly marvellous. When we drive past the health centre he now laments "Doctors, Doctors," proof again he identifies with the building. At school he goes round saying "point five mils Risperidone morning and night," a reference to the fact he has heard us say it to his teachers.

Radio is one of Christopher's greatest past times for he loves listening to songs and adverts and then repeats them all verbatim. It is amazing how he can repeat an advert including the phone number and the web site with the same fluency as a normal person. What I do question is whether any of us just listening to a radio station could take in information from adverts with such ease.

He listens as stories are read at school such as "Upside down Mary Brown" and "The ginger bread man" and takes us all by surprise with a rendition which is word perfect. Almost perfect is his rendering of "Cold Play" and a good few other pop songs, which he has stored away in his memory bank. He has always had the ability to remember the names of fellow class members and at the lodge where he stays for four nights, where there is a considerable number of staff he calls out all of their names in the morning.

It is absolutely amazing that he can over hear you say something, store it for days, sometimes weeks and then come out with it, one has to be very careful these days just what you do say within earshot of this incredible memory man.

Chapter 20
Food Glorious Food

In the last chapter I brushed a little on food, referring to Christopher's outbursts whenever we drive close to a MacDonald's, a chip shop or an ice-cream van and his insistence that he has what he wants and when he wants it.

It hasn't always been like that, in fact it is probably only about the last six months that he has decided to eat a full McDonald's meal, it used to be just the chicken nuggets and it has certainly only been a few months that he has had the urge to eat chips. As a baby Christopher ate the same food as us, all liquidised to start off with and then moving on to more adventurous meals but never refusing them. It wasn't until the autism kicked in that we had a problem, a major problem because he suddenly went from eating well to a child that was refusing virtually everything that was put in front of him. Chris is a very sensory child and will only eat textured foods and you always know when he is enjoying it because he hums as he is eating. It is because of his very poor diet that he always looks so pale and if his sugar level drops he becomes lifeless in the mornings.

For so long Christopher lived on dry cereal for breakfast, dry crackers at lunchtime and then chicken nuggets for dinner in the evening. Just imagine how frustrating and worrying it has been for us as parents never really knowing if your child is hungry or not and most certainly not taking on board enough nourishment each day. We tried vitamin tablets that looked like sweets but he would smell them and throw them away, we bought bottles of omega three fish oil to no avail as he flatly refused to take any drink that we had used to disguise it, to be honest we just did not know what to try next. Even the liquid vitamin and tonic drink was rejected, spat out if we actually managed to get it inside his mouth. Then we saw an advert on an American television channel, you know one of those that just sell different things all day long. We don't usually watch anything like this but just happened to be flicking through the channels and heard someone mention about vitamins in natural fruit juice. We watched and listened with interest, as the lady happened to mention the benefits the machine could bring to a family if they had children that would not eat fruit. Hey, that was us, we listened some more and watched with interest as the woman demonstrated the art of turning about a dozen fresh oranges and a cabbage leaf into what looked a really nice drink. Then it was apples, peaches and various other fruits and unlike the oranges these did not even need peeling. The cabbage leaf was added to provide extra iron and vitamins without changing the look of the drink.

This was perhaps an answer to our problems, "Please stop talking and tell us how much." It seemed like hours but eventually the lady provided the shock to our system, "All of these drinks can be yours, the machine to change your life style, most of it can be cleaned in the dishwasher," then finally and not before time she announced, "And for just one hundred and twenty nine pounds." Now I tell you we badly wanted this machine but well over one hundred pounds, we were not sure if we could afford it at the time. We hesitated and then realised that no matter how much this machine was we had to buy one, it was perhaps the first real break through in providing Christopher with many of the things his body so badly needed.

For the next week or so we had to pull the purse strings in but our heavy-duty juicer was on route from the States. After nearly three weeks this pretty big parcel arrived and we opened it like excited little kids, with a birthday or Christmas present. Tina sent me packing down to the shop to get some fruit and very soon we were ready for the switching on ceremony. Impressive, it was brilliant and still runs regularly in our kitchen today taking only a couple of minutes to turn a dozen oranges into a delicious fruit drink. We started slowly with Chris and he will still only take a glass when he wants to but it has proved to be such a valuable tool in our ongoing fight to feed and water our son. If you find yourself in a similar situation perhaps you would like to know how we manage to get our fruit, rather than pay full price at a supermarket. Most weeks I go either to the local car boot sale, where there's a market or to the market in town and I have made a point of finding out who runs the stalls and have told them why I want the fruit. I leave it fairly late in the day and most times there is quite a bit of fruit still left that probably will not sell and that certainly will not keep too much longer, so the guys are only too pleased to let me have it for a knock down price. It really doesn't matter if it is over ripe in places, in fact with certain fruits such as pineapple, its better. With a deal completed it's off home, get out the "Yankee Wonder," as we have nick named it and turn the lot into a healthy drink, sometimes mixing the fruits just for a change. We do our bit for recycling here as well for we store it in empty plastic milk containers and keeping it refrigerated it lasts for several days.

Even with our new gadget in place Chris still would not change his daily routine of dry cereal, dry crackers and chicken nuggets, we still had to find the answer to this very worrying problem. Some days he would only eat maybe one, sometimes two of the nuggets and then crush the remainder to pieces, sometimes chew them and spit them back into his hand and then launch it like a missile. I know this sounds disgusting but I have to tell you, sometimes instead of throwing them any distance he would aim them for your dinner plate, a lesser person would have been put off their food. We must find an answer not only to Chris's poor diet but also to his manners whilst at the table.

It had been suggested to us that the Intensive Intervention Team might just be able to help, anything was worth a try and so Tina and I agreed to give them a go. Two very pleasant ladies came along several times whilst we were having our meals and observed what went on, perhaps a bit daunting having strangers watching you eat but if we were going to sort Chris out it had to be done. During their visits they made various suggestions that might help, one being to use more photographs to help Christopher. The idea was not just to put chicken nuggets on the table but perhaps on a separate plate a small piece of food the same as we were eating then by having photos of both choices let him decide what he wanted. He always went for the nuggets but did sometimes play with the food on the other plate. Another suggestion, again one we have adopted to this day, was not to put all of the nuggets on one plate. Bring five or six nuggets to the table in a dish and let Chris use a photo to request one of them. Having made his request the nugget would be put on his plate and he would not be allowed to take another until that one was finished. In fact the only difference now is that instead of using a photograph Chris is able to verbally make his request. It is a little annoying when you are trying to enjoy your meal but because of the advances we have made it is well worth hearing him every minute or so saying, "Take one Then," and he will keep this up until you reply.

The only other things one could get Chris to eat in the early days were of course sweets, no child refuses them, chocolate leading to chocolate biscuits and that's about it I think. Gradually though and strangely coinciding with a change of schools Christopher has become more adventurous with his choice of food. First it was a move to foods textured similarly to the nuggets, bread crumbed turkey shapes, chicken drummers to name but two. Since then progress has seen him tackle onion rings, pancakes with syrup on them and packets of sultanas and raisins.

A major discovery was made when I was enjoying my breakfast one morning and had some toast with honey. With nothing to lose I put a small amount of honey on my finger and offered it to Chris. No joy at first but after persevering for a while, well in honesty I sort of stuck a fair bit on his lips, he took the bait and he now absolutely loves the stuff. This was fantastic because it made an opening to introduce various different things to have with the honey, crusty bread, ryvita biscuits, ginger bread men and honey on his pancakes instead of the golden syrup. Something we have to thank the lodge for is getting |Chris to have milk on his cereal these days, what a relief that is and coupled with him drinking milk shakes it means he is getting his daily intake of calcium.

If I told you he was actually eating sausages these days I don't suppose that would really surprise you, but if I said he was eating low fat pork and apple sausages and some with herbs and spices you might be as astonished, as we were when he took his first bite. Now it is nothing for him to eat several of these savoury sausages at one sitting, the record so far being six, only sausages mind, he still will not eat anything else with them. Another shock came only a week or two back when we were cooking fish cakes for Charlie and as Chris seemed really interested, going to the plate and smelling and touching them, we thought why not try him and low and behold, he had done it again, taken us by complete surprise.

Chapter 21
Before Dawn To Well After Dusk

One could almost get away with saying twenty four hours in the life of Christopher for some days it seems exactly like that. I am going to try to remember everything that went on yesterday to give you an idea just how our days are when Chris is home from school.

We always try our best to be awake before Christopher if we can and that way we can normally prevent him from doing any art work, on himself, the walls and the floor. "Oh God," Tina says, "there's the banging he has beaten us to it again." Hardly surprising as we didn't get back to bed until just before three thirty, but that was the day before let me concentrate on yesterday. I'll just tell you that Chris has been in pain from an abscess and has been waking most nights when his pain killer has worn off, somewhere between one and two thirty, more on this in another chapter. So he has done his "Bum Rapp" on the padded door, at least one of us has to get up or pay the consequences. Oh, the time, yesterday it was ten past five when we heard him but it can range any when from four thirty through to about seven. Seven that's right, that's a lay in for Tina and myself but I bet you if by some stroke of luck Christopher sleeps in late little Charlie will decide to wake up early.

So, like a zombie, just after five yesterday morning, I crawled towards Christopher's room wondering what I might find. To my surprise he hadn't performed, although from the smell he may well have been at the planning stage, what should I do next. Chris was screaming for a drink and stickers, yes stickers at five o'clock, I had to make a decision; go get his drink and a biscuit or change him. From experience I know that if he doesn't get his drink quickly he will scream so loud that everyone else is disturbed so off I went downstairs for his hot chocolate. Now in the time it took to warm some milk and stir in some drinking chocolate, then get myself back up the stairs he had made me at least another hours work. He had opened his bowels, torn off his sleeping clothes and spread the mess everywhere, all over himself and his room. Some people who own dogs may think it a bit of an indignity having to pick up their pets mess but trust me if you are one of those people you are getting off very lightly. Even when armed with rubber gloves, a mop and gallons of disinfectant you come out of his room feeling dirty, you have to take a shower yourself. I'm actually lucky to have a wife who has far better hearing than me and very often she has sorted Chris out before I am aware he's even awake but yesterday it just happened to be me.

Chris had created his latest work of art, smiled at me when I came back with his drink and now having taken his refreshment had to be guided downstairs to the bathroom. Just getting him there is a difficult task, stopping him putting his hands on the walls, the doors or even yourself, I'm always relieved if we arrive safely. I think I told you earlier, before we had a shower fitted it was even worse as we had to always give him two baths, one to get the muck off and the second to get rid of the smell. At least now it's much better, bung him in, not literally, scrub him down, again not literally, dry him off and get him back upstairs, making sure of course that he doesn't run back in his room and get messed up again. What we normally do is encourage him to sit with a toy or some stickers, in the spare bedroom, right opposite his and then keep dodging your head round the door to see he is not up to any more mischief.

It is actually easier if both of us tackle the problem and we do more often than not, but if one can get back to sleep and re-charge the batteries then we do. With both on duty, one cleans Chris the other tackles the room but yesterday it was my call, I had drawn the short straw if you like.

Not to worry, Tina and I have been through this so many times now it has become more of a ritual, we just get on with it. Smell! What smell, what mess? Just get it done then you can have a drink yourself and take an early breakfast.

Actually cleaning Chris's room is at least so much easier now than it used to be with the bare walls. It's just a case of clearing out the bedclothes, they have to be changed because they are always messed up or torn up, sweep up the shredded nappy and any other lumps laying around and finally scrub, wash and dry both the walls and the floor. I nearly forgot actually to mention the ceiling for you must check up there first before any lumps have a chance to fall on your head. So that's it, all cleaned up and ready for the day ahead, the time by now getting near to seven.

To broaden Christopher's diet we always give him a choice of what he would like for breakfast, offering at least three cereals but yesterday was just like the day before and the day before that "Tigers." Tigers, that's Crunchy nut cornflakes, in case you're wondering, he comes up with nicknames for most of the packets on offer. Ordinary cornflakes, now they are "Chickens," simply because there is a picture of a chicken on the box, get the idea. Having decided what he wants he looks on, almost with excitement and like a person who hasn't eaten for days whilst we serve it up. You see since his medication was changed to Risperidone he eats like a horse so much so that we have had to keep a strict eye on his weight gain. Once sat at the table we take the opportunity to give him his first medication of the day and get his clothes out ready. It's not long before you hear the cry, "More Tigers," or "Last One," both of which mean to Chris can I have some more. We normally meet his request but make sure that there are far less Tigers in his second bowl, the reason being that it keeps him happy. He has got into the habit of having two bowls, so for the sake of a quiet life we comply, what difference does it make to us whether he has one large portion or two smaller ones, we are just delighted that generally these days he starts the day off right.

Yesterday, I decided to have a bowl of cereal myself and like a fool left it on the table too long. I was sat eating it when Chris demanded his second portion and bear in mind autistic children really do not know the meaning of the word wait, so off I went to the kitchen to recharge his bowl only to find on my return that he had torn up some bits of paper and put them into my bowl. Not so bad I suppose, for other times it might have been worse than paper or the whole thing tipped over the floor. Why is it you leave your food on the table and leave the room, it's because so much is going on you just forget. That's why it is probably wiser to wait and take your breakfast later when Chris has finished and away from the table, trouble is if you take this option you very often get so engrossed in watching him, waiting for his next move, you forget to have breakfast altogether.

Dressing Christopher can sometimes be a simple two or three-minute task or it can take forever, it all depends on his mood.

Well yesterday was one of those days where he had decided to make us work for it, dashing around the room, knocking down a couple of piles of clean clothes all neatly folded and ready for putting away and then he charged back up stairs to annoy his brother.

By this time Tina had come to my aid so there were two of us but that doesn't matter to Chris, there could be an army, he would still take them on. Eventually we completed our mission and being a beautiful morning we took him out to the garden so he could burn off some of his energy on the trampoline. It also gave us the chance to multi task and save a little bit of time. Tina took the opportunity to put the washing on the line and I fed and watered the rabbits, both of us being in positions where we could keep a good eye on our little chap.

Of course when you run your own business it sometimes means you have to do some work when the boys are at home, especially if you have had hospital appointments for the children or yourselves during the week. That being the case this week, we decided that yesterday we would have to complete our deliveries, no orders out means no money coming in and when you are on a tight budget you have little choice. Christopher did not see it that way, he was quite happy bouncing up and down on the trampoline and when we told him we were going to the car he gave us a right run-around. It was fun to him watching us both dodge around the outside of his safe circle knowing if he stayed in the middle we had little chance of catching him, that is without a trick or two of our own. Naughty though it may seem I just mentioned a certain "M" word and he took the bait, following us quickly up the garden, through the house and out to the car. All I was hoping for was a lapse in Christopher's memory that meant he would forget about me mentioning McDonald's. Not our lucky day with that one because he just started shouting out the word from the moment we drove off but not his lucky day either because I chose my route carefully, even if it meant I had to detour a little to avoid any of the happy meal outlets. Deliveries done it was back home for dinner and whilst I prepared the roast, Sunday you see, Tina took both boys back out to the garden to build up their appetites.

So here we were about half way through the day enjoying roast chicken whilst Chris had his sausages cooked on "Old George." That's Chris's name for the George Foreman grill we have recently acquired to take the place of the deep fat fryer that was despatched to the dump, all in the interest of health and safety.

Bearing in mind that Chris eats nothing with them some days he will eat five to six sausages but yesterday it was only three and a half. Here's where you need to be on the alert because if he's had enough he tends to break what is left into tiny little pieces and throw it at you but thankfully this time round he was in a very calm mood and for once sat nicely whilst we finished our meal. Dinner over it was time to at least try and relax and on a Sunday this means Tina and I trying to catch up with East Enders. He may have been good at the table but our Chris can change quicker than you can click your fingers, he was having no sitting around and started by grabbing the left over gravy and pouring it all over the worktop and floor and then made his escape to the garden, straight away climbing onto the trampoline. His insistence to stay in the garden meant that our hour in front of the telly had to be abandoned, out came the chairs on the patio from where we could supervise.

It wasn't long before boredom set in for Chris and he happened to find our few lovely strawberry plants, all laden with fruit, which he pulled off and threw over the fence into the neighbour's garden.

We had one hell of a job trying to get him back in the house. He was determined not to come in and to avoid capture once again took to the safety of the trampoline. In the end we used a ploy similar to the McDonald's trick. On Sundays we normally go to my sisters for tea and Tina had only to mention that we were going to Auntie Daw Daws, that's Christopher's version of Doreen, and he was indoors in a flash. Daw Daws means two things to Chris, jelly and cakes, mind actually getting him from the car into her bungalow nearly always means you arrive feeling exhausted, yesterday being no exception. There may be the nice food but Christopher is also well aware that his auntie and uncle have a Jack Russell dog and as you have heard earlier Chris is terrified of our four legged friends.

The routine we have worked out of late is for Charlie to run on up the garden path and check that Tom is put away in the bedroom whilst Tina and myself struggle in with Chris, sometimes having to revert to carrying him. Once the back door is opened he makes one mad dash for the carver chair at the end of the table and perches himself on the arms and back and generally that is where he stays until we leave. Once in position he starts shouting for the first course, his jelly and knocking that back pretty quickly calls for another. First course over it's on to the cakes and then a drink, which if it is not to his liking, he pours it over the floor. We were lucky yesterday; he must have been particularly thirsty as he sunk his lemonade in one, unusual because he is not particularly fond of fizzy drinks, preferring squash or milk shake.

We are always on edge at my sisters simply because you cannot predict when Christopher may strike, perhaps throwing a cup at the welsh dresser filled with ornaments, grabbing something fragile from the window sill near to where he sits or grabbing something on the way out, just as he did a few weeks ago when he nonchalantly swept a really lovely vase full of beautiful flowers on to the floor, breaking it to pieces. We always feel embarrassed but Doreen has become so understanding of Chris and his habits that she just brushes incidents like this to one side. Thankfully our latest visit passed without any major incidents.

Back home it was time again for Chris to have his medication. Now sometimes he can be as good as gold whilst on other days he will make it extremely hard for you. So with the syringe loaded Tina called out to him and his reaction was to hide behind the sofa, making really horrible screeching noises. The best way to deal with this is for each of us to go to a different end of the sofa, meaning he has no escape. He still doesn't always give in there, like yesterday when we managed to get the syringe into his mouth only to watch him spit most of the dose straight back out. The problem with this is that you do not know how much he has taken and therefore dare not repeat the dose for fear of him having too much. As always we conceded defeat and ushered him to the bathroom, let him have a good old soak and then dressed him ready for bed. Even when Christopher has taken a full dose of his risperidone we know he will not settle straight away so for the next hour or so we always encourage him to sit quietly with one of us, maybe watching the telly or like this Sunday Tina read him a story, made his hot chocolate drink and gave him a couple of ryvitas with honey for his supper, then it was up the wooden hill to bed.

With Christopher's bedroom right opposite our office I tend to use the next couple of hours working at the computer, interrupted from time to time either by his requests for stickers or if he is in a bad mood his consistent screeching. Last night was not too different, I was lucky it was the sticker routine but then after about an hour came the two-minute warning. "You stink," he shouted and that is

97

a warning you ignore at your peril, he is basically letting you know he has messed himself and if you don't sort him out pretty quickly you could finish up having to bath him over again and clean up his room. I was again lucky last night as Tina was also upstairs packing Chris's case in readiness for his return to school today and it was she who came to the rescue. Whilst all of this was going on little Charlie had taken his bath and he too then enjoyed a cuddle with his mum, sometimes it's with dad. This is a very important part of the day, for Tina or myself to fully focus on just him. Many people do not realise that when you have a child as severe as Christopher that your other children do tend to miss out, it is difficult to find Prime Time to spend with them. Every child should have prime time with its parents; it is their right to demand it.

With Christopher now safely tucked up in his room and Charlie resting quietly it was time for Tina and myself to catch up on all of the household chores that had gone undone, not because we were lazing, because we just did not have time to do them whilst the kids are up and about. Tina started at the kitchen, first job she got the washing machine loaded, then the washing up, followed by cleaning the worktops and mopping the floor. Whilst my dear wife did her part I hoovered through the rest of the rooms downstairs and by about ten fifteen we both sat back and enjoyed a glass of wine, the day nearly over. We always try to be in bed by eleven or so because we know from experience that if we don't get at least a couple of hours sleep then we may not get any at all. Last night I suppose we had been asleep nearly three hours, looking at the clock it was just before two, when our early alarm clock sounded. You've guessed it; Chris was banging his door and screeching as loud as he could. Both still feeling dead beat, we dragged ourselves out of bed and over to his room and even before opening the door we knew from the smell that he had donned his Picasso hat yet again. There was mess everywhere over the floor and walls and there wasn't much of himself that he had missed. These episodes have in fact been somewhat worse since he has had the problem with his teeth, waking almost every night for the last two weeks and screaming for his mummy, his only way to express the pain.

In keeping with Christopher's repeated request for mummy's attention, Tina took him off to the bathroom whilst I put on the marigolds and set about cleaning his room. By about ten to three both Chris and his room had a freshness and sparkle about them and we both had job satisfaction. As luck would have it Chris gave up his fight to stay awake fairly soon after he got back to his room and we were able to resume our beauty sleep but how long would it be before he called us on duty again. To our shock and surprise it was ten to eight when we woke this morning, no alarm had been set last night, I was probably too tired. It was in fact a fortuitous phone call from my sister that woke Tina and myself followed just a few minutes after by the bang, bang, bang we have become so accustomed to.

So there you have it, just a normal day in our lives, a life we have come to accept but one we fear that is not recognised by the powers that could still do much more to make not just our lives, but also the lives of all families affected by autism somewhat more comfortable.

Chapter 22
Time to Re-Charge

I have just been talking about help and support that we all need but what does that really mean? Let's not beat about the bush it means, knowing that someone cares, having time available to spend with your other children and indeed with each other, just for a while being able to be like a normal family, it means Respite.

Of course there are those people that might think a parent that accepts respite for their child is being selfish, only thinking of themselves but through this chapter I hope to show how just a little break here and there can make the world of difference. It is said "The Lord Giveth and The Lord Taketh Away," and to be honest it is not too much different with the authorities that can with a snap of the finger improve your lives or make things very much harder for you. Since Christopher was diagnosed we have not been given any respite without first having to fight for it, no one has come along and said life must be hard for you, here is some time off.

I have said it on so many occasions and still maintain that whilst most of the professionals associated with child care, whether it be social or medical, are brilliant people none can truly understand the anguish, the heartache and the day to day struggle parents have with their lives and family that is affected by the invasion of autism.

Before telling you about the respite we have had for Chris and what we are trying to achieve at present and for the future let me try to paint a picture how having an autistic son has affected us financially.

As you have already read it was necessary for me to give up the driving school and we have not been able to work Tina's business as hard as we would have liked. Try convincing me that anyone can maintain the same standard of life when they suddenly have their income chopped in half. My title is, "Tell it as it is" and that is exactly what I have done thus far but if there hasn't been anything to shock you up to now how about living in fear of losing your home? Twice we have really struggled to keep up with our mortgage payments but with the threat of eviction hanging over us we have battled on. Tina and myself have gone without but never compromising the lives of our children. Yes, they have had clothes that are second hand but never have they gone hungry. Our struggle for survival has meant that we have not been able to throw our money around on classy holidays but through it all we have learnt to value what we have and fight for what we want. Many couples would have buckled but the bond between Tina and myself, the will to win and the ambition to achieve greater things for our children has kept us going. Hopefully, if you are one of the people who have found it hard to conceive why respite should hold such an importance in our lives then I will have reached a nerve or opened your eyes to something that can truly make a difference. Just an odd day here or there where one could simply relax, forget the egg shell syndrome and give one hundred per cent of your time, energy and love to the others in your family.

It is never easy in today's financial climate to get respite for your child and we had to really push hard to achieve what we were given. Of course there were all sorts of interviews and meetings to ascertain whether Christopher and our circumstances warranted the respite care.

We stuck by our guns throughout and eventually we were granted one Wednesday night every other week with a view to building on this in the future. Christopher was collected by a carer from his school and taken directly to the centre where he would enjoy tea, playtime and then sleep over, returning directly to school in the morning. I do not mean to sound ungrateful but being mid week there was little we could do with Charlie, particularly as the nights drew in and winter approached. Never mind, we thought, it was the thin end of the wedge; if we were patient we might eventually be given weekends. True to their word the centre finally told us they had a weekend vacancy and asked if we would like to accept. This was worth having as Chris was picked up from school by the centre on Friday afternoon and did not return home until he had finished school the following Monday, finally we had a chance to spend some time with our other little boy and of course chill out a little. Before you get carried away I have to point out that this award was not every week, it was one weekend a month and it also meant we lost the Wednesday respite. It took a lot of getting used to; not having Chris around, doubts crept in as to whether we were doing the right thing. Once we had it clear in our heads that Chris was safe and well looked after I think the tension eased and we used many of the weekends to great use.

One of the ladies looking after Chris at the respite centre once said to my wife, "I look after your son, bath him, care for him but at least at the end of my shift I can go home." That is the difference for when you are looking after someone as difficult as Christopher day after day it takes its toll, respite is so important. Time to just take a break, have a lie in or just eat a meal without any stress.

One weekend a month was very little in truth and so we started to campaign for a little bit more and again after many meetings the funding was found so that we could have five hours break each Sunday, which seemed fine until we had to argue for more funds when a risk assessment was completed and showed that Chris needed two to one care. He had started to get very aggressive towards the lady who took him out on a Sunday, sometimes to a play centre, other times to a park and some Sundays she took him swimming. He had started to damage her car and he really needed an extra person to sit next to him to keep him amused and focus his attention away from the naughty things he was doing. We have our social worker to thank for a fairly prompt and positive response to our request, which meant from then on he would have the extra carer. It was not always the same person that made up the extra escort and Chris took full advantage of anyone new, attacking and biting them whenever he could. Nevertheless they were all pretty good with him and never made a serious complaint.

I have to pay special tribute to his main carer Karen who built up a fantastic understanding relationship with Chris and when the respite came to an end she was extremely upset. For weeks after Christopher would call out her name and I am sure he was more than a little confused why he was not going out on a Sunday morning.

Christopher was also invited to attend a club which was run fortnightly on Saturday mornings for an hour and a half, all we had to do was convince social services to fund it, which thankfully they did. So overall we had five hours on a Sunday, an hour and a bit every other week and one week end a month to do exactly what we wanted to with Charlie. The weekends were also very useful to us as three times a year we had company conferences and with the co-operation of the respite centre manager we were able to link Christopher's respite and enjoy a weekend in Birmingham amongst friends and colleagues whilst Charlie stayed with his sister and had great fun.

These weekends away were not just about work, they gave Tina and myself time for each other, time to relax and time to recharge our batteries. If you have an autistic child, particularly one that is on the severe end of the spectrum, you must have a break, time off from scraping mess off of walls, from chasing your child all over the house, time to be normal again.

They say all good things come to an end. Go back to what I said at the start of this chapter, about giving and then taking away. How is it? Give with the right hand and take away with the left, something like that anyway. That is what happened to us when we successfully got Chris into his new school, where he would stay for four nights and return home on a Friday. You'll read later about our joy when we received the letter of confirmation, joy that soon turned to tears and anger when the very next day we received a phone call to tell us that we had lost all other respite save that of the Saturday mornings.

It had been concluded that as we would have four nights free we did not need any respite at weekends but what had been overlooked was the real reason for having time on a Saturday and Sunday, to spend special time with little Charlie, which we had done with the exception of three weekends a year. If we were to spend prime time with him and take him to places of enjoyment should we assume that we take him out of school or perhaps take him out in the evenings when he should be doing homework and getting to bed at a reasonable time. One thing is for sure that we are certainly no better off from a social aspect.

A part of our business involves training people in our team and once a month we held a meeting in Winchester for that purpose. We were very fortunate because one of the ladies working at the respite centre had her hours cut and she very kindly offered to look after Christopher and Charlie whilst we were at our meeting. You see one cannot leave a child like Chris with an ordinary baby sitter, they need special skills and as Angie had many years experience dealing with autistic children it was ideal. Of course if you employ someone with specialist skills you have to pay more for them.

It was fine for several months but when we were told Christopher really needed two to one care we could no longer afford to keep our meetings going. Not only did we miss out on vital time with our team but also the refreshing break that we got from the evening. Many of our family have helped in the past but only recently Christopher proved too big a handful for them. We had just gone out for about two hours to Charlie's band concert and on return found that Chris had pulled the curtains down in the lounge.

We cannot even have a holiday again this year, having been turned down for twenty-four hour respite just for a few days on the grounds that we are being selfish and not allowing our son Christopher to integrate with his family. We have been granted ten whole days, but no nights, that's actually six whole hours a day, so tell me where can we take our other son in that time. Perhaps we should look at it that we are having ten holidays this year albeit very short ones. Why I ask are parents with children of any disability ostracised, are we not entitled to have a holiday? A holiday is deemed to be a break from the rigours of your life that you endure for the rest of the year. If we take Chris away do you really think he is going to benefit?

As parents we know from experience he will spend the whole of the time screeching, unhappy that he is not in familiar surroundings why are things like this not considered when decisions are made. We love our son very dearly and would give anything to be able to book a holiday, to take him with us and all have a wonderful relaxing time, but unless Christopher improves beyond all recognition it will just never happen. So for us it is no more weekends away at our conferences, our only chance to truly enjoy being a couple and our dreams of ever taking our family to Florida have surely been blown away.

Never mind it is our ambition to work hard in the time available and save as hard and for as long as it takes to buy our own motor home, have it converted to suit Christopher's needs, and once he feels comfortable and used to the inside we hopefully won't have to bother anyone.

Until then I guess it means that whilst those who make the decisions enjoy their one or two holidays a year we shall have to make do with going to "Argate."

Argate you wonder, oh that's down the end of our garden.

Chapter 23
I'm All Right Jack

If you happen to be a parent with a disabled child may I ask you a question? Have you ever stopped and thought to yourself whether anyone really cares about you and your family? Maybe the professionals you encounter throughout your child's life, your family, your friends or just Jo Public.

I'll go into that in just a moment but please let me make something very clear to you, whether people care or whether they don't need not make the slightest bit of difference to you. If you have the right attitude and the inner strength these need not worry you at all. I say that but for a long time Tina and I were worried, not just whether people cared but what they thought of us and our family. That has all changed; I can assure you, we have worked hard to improve our attitude towards life throughout our journey with autism and as a result are far stronger people.

Yes, there are people in this world who are very self centred, there are professionals out there who shut out your problems once the five o'clock buzzer sounds, we have experienced some of them but have learned that they are in the minority. Let me assure you that for every one of these that might enter your life at sometime, you will be more than compensated by the many thousands of wonderful understanding and caring people who are willing to listen, who are prepared to help and at the very least give you the time of day.

When we first found out about Christopher we went through a period of mourning, almost in the same way as one would if your child had died. Probably the most poignant moment in this period of our lives was when we realised that he could not communicate with us, that feeling of hopelessness not being able to ask for a drink. The moment our little boy poured a bottle of milk over the floor and then got down and lapped it up, replicating an animal, we had lost him forever.

It is said that time is a great healer. Time alone would not however help us to accept that having witnessed that agonising episode that there could possibly be any future for our little boy or indeed us as parents. If you are a parent going through this period of mourning yourself or perhaps have been through it already and cannot see light at the end of the tunnel please take heart from how Tina and I dealt with the problem.

Christopher was our son, with or without autism and we loved him dearly. We realised that henceforth we were his voice; it was up to us to fight his corner and for this to happen we had to change our outlook on life. We were no good to our son if all we did was to spend the rest of our days feeling sorry for ourselves, blaming others or worrying what they thought. What mattered then and still matters today is our son's future. So far it has been a bumpy road, we have had to work hard to get Chris the best, never willing to accept anything less, we deleted the word procrastination from our vocabulary but you know by doing these things mourning has been replaced by rejoicing. Rejoicing in the remarkable progress that our little boy has made and constantly celebrating as another step on that never ending ladder is climbed.

One hears of couples that have an autistic child, or perhaps a child with another disability, ending their marriage, the pressure becoming too much for one of the partners and that is so very sad. The strength that Tina and I have achieved by adopting a positive attitude, by forming a very unique togetherness, by devoting our lives to our family and not being prepared to give up on our quest for Christopher has been paramount in making our lives together so worth while. It could have been so different, we could have given in, accepted just what happened to come our way but we chose otherwise. I tell you, I really do not care if I come across one of the" I'm All Right Jack, Blow You" type of people, they no longer worry me nor do they have any influence on my life.

Chapter 24
Help I Need Somebody

In the last chapter I told you not to worry about what people say and not to worry if you come across a person or organisation that is not willing to help. Move on and find the people that will give their time and a listening ear to your problem.

Before Tina and myself started our journey through the autistic maze I have to admit that I was very much Anti social workers. Without going into too much detail let me just say that a certain young lady refused to listen to my concerns about the safety of a very young child that my first wife and I were fostering. After increasing evidence came to light when the child made various home visits I was still not being listened to and therefore was forced to go over the social workers head and from that time lost faith in certain members of the system. Thank God a senior member of staff took my concerns seriously and the little girl was protected from more harm.

As Christopher's problem hit home it became increasingly more obvious that we perhaps could do with some help and we decided after talking to social services to accept their offer of help and support. I must say I made it perfectly clear that having had the previous encounter it was very much on our terms, Tina and I did not want someone to take over, just to point us in the right direction to find the help we needed. I told you very early on in this book that the social worker assigned to help us was a very bubbly young lady, nothing being too much trouble and with only one goal in mind, to support and improve both Christopher's and our life styles. So if you are in a similar situation to us, maybe just starting out on your family's autistic journey, don't suffer in silence. Swallow any pride you may have, make a call and share your problems. Do remember that if you are not happy with a person you must be brave enough to ask for a change, it is no good trying to work with anyone in whom you have no confidence.

So who are the people and the organisations that we have turned to for support or financial assistance along the way? The first and probably the most important as far as finance goes is the department for Disability Living Allowance, which as many of you will know is split into two parts, the care side and the mobility element. The rates for both of these are relative to the disability your child has, a lower rate for moderate cases and a higher rate for those at the top end of the scale. There is also a middle rate for the care component, which is what we were given when we first applied. Thankfully we were guided very wisely by our social worker who told us to appeal and include the words, Severely, Mentally, Impaired. These three words were key to us getting the higher rate for both elements. Please remember if you need to claim to include these three vital words when you describe your child, never lie but paint the blackest picture of the worst day you can remember. We took our time over completing the forms and although it seemed as if we were answering the same questions over and over again we persevered to make sure there could be no doubt about the severity of our sons illness. Like us, you may also be eligible for Carers allowance and although this is means tested it is well worth the effort if you happen to qualify.

Qualification for help from an organisation known as the Family Fund also depends on your income, together with your circumstances overall. After contacting them we were interviewed by a lovely lady and were eventually accepted for a grant. The society has helped us with a washing machine, bedding, clothing and the year we went to Gran Canaria they were kind enough to help with a small grant towards the cost.

If you are one of those persons that find filling out forms difficult it is worth remembering a charity called The Parent Partnership, run by volunteers, some of who are parents of disabled children themselves. You may have one in your area.

They have been extremely helpful to us, not just with forms but also educational appeal procedures.

There is of course the National Autistic Society and if you are lucky like us we have a local society called The Hampshire Autistic Society. Both of these are very supportive and there is always someone available to lend an ear. Of course being charities these great organisations are always glad of help so whether you are like us with a disabled child or someone who is just interested in lending a hand rest assured a very warm welcome awaits you. I know there have been times when we have felt ostracised, not necessarily because other people have left us out, although this has happened, but because we have found it hard to speak with others. I think it helped when we got ourselves involved in small local help groups and I am sure there will be something like that wherever you live. If you cannot find any information on these then perhaps it would be a good idea to ask your health visitor or at your doctors surgery. I hope British Telecom will forgive me for using one of their much-used phrases, remember, "It's good to talk."

I could go on to list many local help groups throughout the United Kingdom but I hope with those that I have mentioned you will have seen that there is help out there, though perhaps not enough. Make sure you claim all that is rightfully yours or your child's and if at first you don't succeed keep on trying. We could all do with more help and support, more funding from the government so please make sure you keep asking. If we all raise awareness of our child's needs who knows our voices might be heard one of these days.

Chapter 25
What the People Think

Until our son was diagnosed with Autism both Tina and myself had very little idea of just what it meant. I believe this to be the case with the majority of the population, not based on their intelligence, or their social standing but because of their ignorance.

I use the word ignorance not in a nasty or rude way but am I not right to assume that unless folks are directly affected by autism or they happen to be professionals in the field they have no reason to comprehend its meaning or implications it can have on families?

In this chapter I want to show you how many different theories members of the public have regarding autism and I asked people from varying walks of life one question, "What is autism?" You will see the results for yourself but before looking at these let me share with you some professional views obtained on the Internet and although most of the theories conform to each other they do also have their own ideas.

"Autism is a brain disorder that begins in early childhood and persists throughout adulthood affecting three crucial areas of development: communication, social interaction and creative or imaginative play."

"Autism is a disorder of the brain function that appears early in life, generally before the age of three. Children with autism have problems with social interaction, communication, imagination and behaviour. Autistic traits persist into adulthood, but vary in severity. Some adults with autism function well, earning degrees and living independently whilst others never develop the skills of daily living and may be incorrectly diagnosed with a variety of psychiatric illnesses. The cause is unknown."

"Autism is a chronic developmental disorder usually diagnosed between eighteen and thirty months of age. Symptoms include problems with interaction and communication as well as repetitive interest and activities. At this time, the cause of autism is not known although many experts believe it to be a genetically based disorder that occurs before birth."

Let me now share with you the thoughts on autism of our local Avon lady who when asked replied "I think autism is when someone has a great difficulty in interacting and communicating with other people, which causes them much frustration, with the result that they lash out and hurt whoever is with them and sometimes they even harm themselves. Sleeping does not come easy either, so looking after them is very exhausting. Special care and schools offer some respite. Medication can help, but researches still do not know its exact cause. I have just watched the news on television where they have been reporting on autistic children. A scientist has made a robot and children seem to be able to interact well with it, copying its movements and smiling, then turning to their carers, as if to say, look what I can do, which is a wonderful thing to see."

I then asked a mum at Charlie's band practice, she told me, " Autism is a form of learning difficulty. The degree of severity varies between each individual. People with autism find communication difficult and they seem unable to understand simple instructions, which often have to be repeated. Routine is important and they can easily become distressed and frustrated."

Another person I asked, a parent at Charlie's school told me, "My experience of autism has been mainly from the media, films such as

Rain Man with Dustin Hoffman. As far as I am aware the condition is neurological and affects each person to varying degrees causing the individual to become withdrawn with emotional and communication difficulties and an obsessive personality."

I happened to mention to my sister just a few days ago that I was hoping to include a chapter which would reflect what other people's ideas of autism might be and to my surprise she has put together the following and I would ask that you forgive her if the grammar is not quite right; one thing is for sure, she has written this as I have written my book, from the heart.

"I am Christopher's Auntie Daw Daw and I know more than most people what life for my brother Charlie and his wife Tina has been like. I just wish I were younger so that I could help them more with Chrissy but as I am nearly seventy and not in good health I just do what I can as they have had a very hard time with Chris. Their friends have all disappeared because they don't want their homes broken up but as I understand the problem I welcome them in my home on Sundays. My attitude is if things get broken they can be replaced, whilst damage to his health and his family cannot be replaced. My husband and I love Chris a lot, as we do all children. We do not push Chris aside because we think he is different. I do wish when people see Chris out and he is playing up that they would just stop and think what may be the real trouble. Not just stand there saying, can't they keep that child under control, as has been said. It is very hard to look after a child like Christopher, please do not judge children like him without first stopping to think."

"It is very hard for Tina and Charlie as they have to work and look after Chris at the same time but never complain, they just take it in their stride. Of course when Chris is very bad they are on edge, they can never ever relax, as they should be able to do from time to time. All parents that look after autistic children deserve a medal, non-more so than my brother and sister in law, not continual criticism from people when they can't keep him quiet. They are always in my prayers, and I hope through my brother writing this book someone out there will understand a little bit more about their problems."

Now I told my sister I was going to ask various people to tell me in their own words, a maximum of fifty what their ideas of autism might be. I am so proud of Doreen writing these two paragraphs and there was no way that I could cut any of her words, I just hope she has in her words endorsed just how difficult life can be for any parent looking after an autistic child.

You might be interested to know that eight people that I asked declined to say anything other than they didn't have a clue about autism. One even admitted that because they weren't affected by it that they were not interested. A fine attitude but sort of proves what I am trying to do within this chapter.

I was lucky enough to catch a bank clerk during her lunch hour and she told me, "I know very little about autism. I believe that there are various levels from mild to severe. A person with the condition has problems interacting with the world around them. For the families the problems are many and have to be dealt with all day every day."

Tina and I recently had the opportunity to spend some time out together, something we rarely get the chance to do these days and we called in to Pococks Rose nursery in Romsey and spent an hour or so taking in the beauty and the fragrances. Roses being Tina's favourite flower I spoiled her with some lovely bushes, one in particular just for her, called "Lovely Lady." There I go again digressing, but whilst there I had the chance to find out what one of the nurserymen knew about autism.

"Autistic children are very intelligent but cannot have a loving relationship. I believe they do not have the ability to be one to one with other children and they can throw really bad tantrums."

A receptionist at the local college told me, "There's all different types of autism and it's something to do with the genes. It's similar to ADHD but more serious. I feel disgusted that more is not done to help."

A business colleague from Devon believes, " A child with autism has little or no understanding of things, which will result in learning difficulties of communicating with other people and they also dislike close contact with people unless it is on their terms."

An elderly lady, Miss Muriel Morse, whom I have had the pleasure of knowing now for some forty-nine years, in fact since I was a young boy, agreed to help proof read my work and also to contribute with her feelings and understanding and wrote the following.

"Charlie came to visit me one evening, he needed to talk to someone and having spent a while chatting I hoped he went away feeling slightly better. It was during our conversation that I started to learn the full implications of extreme autism. How could I not be affected? It was only much later that I realised there was another very venerable person involved. How could young Charlie survive unharmed by his brother's disability? Could he remember the days of normal family life? Mum and Dad were, by circumstances, forced to give so much attention to Christopher so wasn't it inevitable that Charlie missed out. How could he invite his friends to the home, not only because of Christopher's threatening behaviour but also because of the smell that all the cleaning air sprays could not dispel? How could a young boy protect his own belongings?"

"I then had the pleasure of meeting Young Charlie and found him to be a very bright, kind and understanding; he is also very good looking, tomorrows Lady Killer. He came with his father to ask if he could use me for a school project about World War Two. He actually asked me to take part in a question and answer interview. His attitude was very mature and organised well beyond his few years. Thank goodness, I thought, for his interest in birds and animals. Having completed the interview the subject turned to dad's book and I volunteered myself to help with the proof reading process."

"Although the family is incomplete for four days of the week, with his brother living at Hope Lodge, little Charlie can now develop as a youngster should. Mum and Dad can now revert to being there for him knowing that Chris is safe and making good progress that was perhaps not possible at home, supported by loving help from specially trained staff who are dedicated to their charges. It makes me wonder how many more siblings are badly in need of help? I would like to conclude by saying well done to young Charlie for the way he has dealt with the situation himself. I know his dream is to become a vet and I hope that one day his dream will come true."

You see, whilst quite a few of the people who have helped with this chapter have a sort of idea about autism, hardly anyone really fully understands the problem or the implications it can have on a family. Take us, until Christopher was diagnosed with autism and we therefore became involved or should I say affected we never turned an eye to a newspaper report relating to the subject. Why? Simply because like so many, when everything was going well, we lived within our own world and cared very little about anyone outside of it. When I look back I do feel ashamed that I didn't take more notice and that is why it is so important for me to raise awareness to the problem of autism today, to make sure that as many people as possible are aware of its presence and I live in hope that some of those people will be prepared to give a little of their time and energy towards such a great cause. This may look as if I am only trying to enlist help because my family needs it but trust me when I say that both Tina and myself intend to work tirelessly towards building a greater awareness world wide and where possible take on tasks that will benefit autistic children.

Finally I would like to conclude this chapter with a poem that my son Charlie has written. He has done this completely on his own in response to my question, "What does autism mean to you son."

My Autistic Brother

Christopher is sometimes nasty
And people get bruises
Sometimes I wish he could understand
But then sometimes he plays with me
Sometimes he makes me laugh
I know he is autistic
But he is always special to me

Especially he likes bath toys
So he can keep himself calm
Sometimes he tries to flood the place
And makes it like the sea
He always likes my company
I know he can't say in his own words
He's saying I love you because you love me

So there you have different opinions on a problem that is affecting more people every year. There are some that have an idea of what autism is but the majority of people find it difficult to describe. More and more children are being diagnosed every year and it seems to me that it is not until people are personally affected that they try to understand. This of course is not their fault but I do think it would help if an effort were made to raise people's awareness to the problems of looking after an autistic child. Awareness not just to the ordinary person in the street but also to our leaders. Let us all speak out and make sure governments through the world know what it is like to be at the coalface.

Chapter 26
Our Greatest Battle

During the past six years or so when autism has had such a devastating affect on my family we had to tackle many issues and climb numerous mountains all of which we tackled with a determination to get the best for our son. We are no different from any other parents determined to see their child succeed and hoping that they will eventually do something useful with their life but of course for an autistic child it is so much harder.

It was therefore vitally important to us that Christopher always has the best possible education that could be provided. In my mind education to an autistic child is not initially about learning to read, write or do sums, it is about teaching them social skills and living in harmony with their peers. Obviously if any of the academic skills follow it is the icing on the cake.

When Christopher first went to his primary school he appeared to be making really great progress, interacting well most of the time and complying with the simple disciplines that were expected. I think his favourite activities were swimming and quiet time in the sensory room where he would listen intensely to soft music whilst enjoying his back or legs massaged. The teacher and classroom assistants all loved Chris, his gorgeous blue eyes and long blond ringlets were features that made him hard to resist.

His first Christmas at the school came around and he made a brief appearance in the nativity celebrations but even then insisted on performing inconspicuously with a blanket over his head. Another year passed, another Christmas and that year he made only a very brief appearance right at the end, which left us wondering why. By that time Christopher was becoming more aggressive and it was clear his autism was getting worse. We had started to receive home bags of torn clothes and shoes and reports that he had begun targeting both staff and pupils alike. Very close to his third Christmas at the school we were called in as he was feeling poorly. On arrival I learnt that a small boy in a wooden support frame had been thrown by Christopher hitting his head in the process and that an ambulance had been called. Just how do you think we felt? Fortunately the lad was all right and didn't need hospital treatment but it could have been much worse.

Tina and myself had been campaigning for Christopher to receive one to one care whilst at school and we hoped that this latest incident would add weight to our argument. When Chris was out on a school trip he was supposed to have two to one care but this was not happening either and was brought to our notice in his school to home diary where we read that he sat down in the middle of a fairly busy road.

The school he was at was good whilst they could cope with Christopher's behaviours but during his last year there it become obvious to us that he had outgrown the school, he needed more specialised care. What Chris needed was experts in the field of autism and we decided that we should immediately start looking for an educational establishment that could cater for all of his needs including one that could help with his diet.

If this meant that we would have to move home then so be it, we would take whatever steps were required to ensure that our son had the very best chance to improve his standard of life. We have friends who live in Dorset and it was they who told us of a specialist autistic school near their home, could it be that we were off down the West Country. Try as we may we could not find any other schools around the area with the attributes that our son needed, save one other in Brighton. Then one day, out of the blue it hit me, Hope Lodge, was it still around? I did another search on the Internet using this time using the school's name and lo and behold it appeared. I felt such a fool, how could I have forgotten that we had just the school in our own town? You see, some twenty years before, whilst working for a local shipbuilder I used to go to Hope Lodge, at the site which is now their residential centre and do little repair jobs on the beds and anything else that was worth repairing. I will always remember a lad lying on his bed as I was drilling the bed frame to fit some brackets. He said "Excuse me, how fast does the armature go round in your drill?" I was amazed; I didn't even know it had one.

So Hope Lodge it was, we had decided but we hadn't figured on getting as much opposition as we did to get Chris accepted. Let me make it clear I do not mean opposition from the school, I mean from the powers to be that have to fund the placement.

The first thing we did was to request a brochure, I know there is a posh name for these things but I can't think of it at the moment. Any way the information turned up in the post after about a week so we had our bedtime reading for a couple of nights. From the prospectus, its just come back to me, we could see that Hope Lodge could be just what we were looking for, a real chance for our son to make serious progress. "Let's not waste any time," I said to Tina, "How do we apply?" The next stage, before any forms were completed was to visit the school and see for ourselves the facilities they had on offer. It was several weeks before the next day arranged for prospective parents to visit and it seemed like an absolute age. Eventually the visiting day arrived and with a feeling of excitement and anticipation we made our way to the school. The Parent Liaison Officer, Barbara, met us at reception and made us feel very welcome and at ease right from the start. We were invited to fire questions at her over coffee and biscuits and then given a guided tour around the school. Without being told one could not help noticing the teacher, pupil ratio, there being almost as many adults around as children. I think the most impressive thing to us was when we were invited in to the dining hall where students were sitting with their teachers and were encouraged to serve themselves, almost in a "Silver Service" manner. This was the deciding factor as far as we were concerned; all we wanted to hear was whether they wanted Chris. Before they could make that decision the head master and a manager from the residential side would need to assess Christopher at his present school.

Our paediatrician had been trying to let us down lightly I think about Christopher's future because she quite often spoke about the possibilities of him being in some sort of residential care by the time he became a teenager. If Hope Lodge were to accept Chris we had a major decision to make. Do we just send him to the school each day or do we apply for residential care four nights a week? Which ever way we decided we knew we would have a real battle on our hands, so would it be better to have one fight right at the beginning or take a chance and apply just for the daytime and then have to go through the whole process again in a few years time.

I can tell you it is probably the most difficult decision Tina and I have ever been asked to make but before we left Hope Lodge that day we indicated that we would more than likely opt for the residential package. I think what helped us eventually was when it was explained in more detail that the idea of the residential, or as they call it, a waking day curriculum, is not just to teach your child whilst at school but to continue showing them social skills throughout the evening.

Having made our minds up that Hope Lodge School was where we wanted Christopher to spend his days in education we were faced with an enormous battle with the local authority to firstly agree that it would be beneficial for our son to change schools and secondly to agree to funding the project. Our next move was to make formal application for them to consider our proposal. We carefully compiled our letter making sure that they were aware of all of Christopher's problems. The fact that the medication he was on did not seem to be enough on its own for Chris to make any progress in the control of his by now violent outbursts. At the same time we wrote to all of the doctors and consultants involved with Chris and asked for their backing.

We also reminded them that there was a risk assessment in place stating that Christopher needed two to one care whilst indoors and two to one care when he went out and that it seemed difficult for his present school to maintain this level. Another very important issue was that a speech and language therapist was no longer available at his school and we felt that was of paramount importance and Hope Lodge provides that facility. Together with the fact that Hope Lodge had special programmes in place to help with eating surely we had a good case?

Just in case there needed to be more evidence we reminded the panel that as Christopher's present school was closing down and moving to temporary premises whilst a new school was built it was far better for him as an autistic child to have one move where he could stay until at least sixteen rather than move twice fairly quickly and then again when he reached senior school age. We also discovered that some of the professionals had already met to discuss Christopher and one had suggested that he stay at his present school and be given fifty two week care, effectively taking over the care of our child. I was absolutely livid, what reason did they have for this, were they trying to say we were bad parents; this was definitely not going to happen. I decided to do some homework and without going into too many details discovered that our proposal would cost something in the region of seventy thousand pounds each year whilst the other totally unacceptable proposal would cost more than one hundred and ninety thousand pounds. Where was the sense in a move like that, it would happen over my dead body?

We had already been told by social services that it was highly unlikely we would get the funding for Christopher to move but we took no notice of that and our letter was sent off on the twenty first of February two thousand and six. I must tell you that there were many other reasons included in our application but one has to be careful what you write.

We were encouraged when our social worker told us that at a "Pre Marps" meeting, that's Multi Agency Revue Panel, most of the attendees appeared to be in favour but then came the crunch.

On the thirtieth of March the main panel met and rejected Christopher's move pending further inquiries and the results of a meeting, which we were invited to attend. Not a meeting of the panel, they meet in secret, I think rather like a Masonic lodge, we are not permitted to meet them and voice our opinions. No, this meeting was with the leader of the educational services, Christopher's present head and deputy head of school, a psychologist, our social worker and as I said ourselves. There was another very important person present and that was a member of the Parent Partnership Group, there to support us and add weight to our argument.

May the second was "D" day, the big show down if you like, an opportunity for Tina and myself to put our case and hopefully that our concerns and consequent request to change schools was justified. We had not taken this meeting lightly, it was do or die for us and for our son's future. We had spent many days preparing a statement that I would read at the meeting. So there we were sitting in this tiny room waiting for the chairman to arrive, it seemed a long time but eventually a gentleman entered the room and introduced himself.

For legal reasons I think it best if I do not go into detail of the discussions but just tell you that my wife and I left the room with a feeling of a job well done. I will tell you that as well as the statement we also tipped out a black bag full of clothes that had been destroyed whilst Chris was at school and I think this had its impact. The battle was not over however, we still had to wait for a final decision from the Marps panel when they reconvened on May the eleventh but we felt quietly confident.

To the credit of the special educational needs department, having said they would ring us on the twelfth of May, they did, contacting me during the day by telephone and without telling Tina she knew the result was in our favour just by the broadest grin that has ever been seen on my face. We were elated, our son was to start at his new school full time in September with a few taster days before the school broke up for the summer.

Elation can so easy turn to sorrow or disappointment. It was the very next day that we received another phone call during which we learnt that we would lose all other respite except an hour or so every fortnight at the Saturday club. This of course was a real blow but what we had achieved greatly outweighed any thing we had lost. In any case we would battle on and still to this day we are determined to fight for anything that might improve life for Christopher, little Charlie and ourselves.

Chapter 27
New Hope

Monday the fourth of September two thousand and six was indeed a very special day for Tina and myself. It was the day of new hope, the day that Christopher started at Hope Lodge School, the day for us all to look forward and hopefully leave the past behind.

We were up early that morning to make sure both the boys had time to eat a good breakfast; Chris had his dried Cheerios, before getting them dressed into their uniforms. Uniform, a first for Christopher, for although he had been at school for nearly three years school uniform was not called for. Chris looked magnificent, dressed in all new clothes, his lovely blue jumper with the Hope Lodge School logo putting the finishing touches. Of course like many parents it was out with the camera to capture that magic moment, Christopher in blue contrasted by his brother Charlie in red.

With both boys at the ready it was just a case of waiting for the taxi to arrive for Christopher, to take him on a journey, which hopefully would be the start of a new era, a chance to make up ground and a real opportunity to improve the way he was coping with his condition. Well we didn't have long to wait, as the taxi was early. It did however seem so strange saying bye bye to our little chap, we just prayed that all would go well. Christopher did not start his residential stay at the Lodge straight away, he just went there for tea, straight from school and then we collected him and brought him home for the night. It was when we got to the Lodge on that first day that we learnt things hadn't gone quite to plan for within half an hour of Christopher arriving at school in his lovely new uniform he had torn the front of the jumper beyond repair. We were not entirely surprised, he was still well into tearing at this stage and he was not going to be converted in just one day. Just so you don't get confused the school is known as Hope Lodge and the place where Chris stays during the week is just known as the Lodge.

Chris continued through out the early weeks at Hope Lodge School to cause lots of problems, carrying on I suppose where he had left off at the previous school. In the first two months there were about thirty incidents recorded where Christopher either attacked staff, pupils or the classroom. Indeed by this time he had also seen off two escorts that were employed to accompany him from home to school and the return journey on a Friday. Just to prove the strength Chris has in his jaw let me tell you that although the first escort had a thick coat on over her arms he managed to bite her in both arms leaving bruises about the size of a digestive biscuit. You're probably not surprised when I tell you that escort never turned up again. The second one who suffered the same fate lasted even less time and we were asked to ferry Christopher to school until they found a suitable replacement. Now either the school transport have conveniently forgotten or word has got out and all available escorts have left town because to this day we are still taking Chris to school ourselves. I know I have mentioned about these escorts earlier and I hope you will excuse me but I think it was important enough to mention again.

The staff at Hope Lodge are always quick to respond to a problem and they wasted no time at all in implementing two very important things that would at last see Chris start to settle.

Firstly they arranged that whilst school was closed over the Christmas period that Christopher's classroom would be completely rebuilt, so that everything could be safely locked away and anything that was easily picked up and could be thrown, like the tables, were fixed down.

Next to the classroom was quite a small room that was adapted just for Christopher when he started to disrupt his fellow classmates. If he started to have a serious tantrum his two key workers would take him to this room and work there until he had shown signs of calming down. To be fair it has worked extremely well and only last week his teacher told us she couldn't remember the last time they used this special room.

The second and most important move towards transforming our son was to introduce two to one care at all times. Even before funding was approved the school viewed this with such importance that they implemented it and then worried about the finance later. Within a very little time Christopher started to conform with class discipline, not all of the time, if he was perfect he probably wouldn't have an autistic label, but there were definite signs that he may have turned the corner. Having the extra pair of hands in the classroom has allowed staff to change around more frequently, a ploy that Christopher responds very well to and one that has been used rather than take him to his room.

Just to prove that all the best-made plans never always run smooth let me tell you about one very frightening moment around the time Sudan Hussein was executed. Christopher was playing quite nicely in the playground with his two support workers keeping a close eye. It was time to go back to the classroom for story time and when told to go inside Chris made a mad dash, taking his teachers by surprise and leaving them a fair way behind. When the teachers entered the classroom they saw Chris standing on a chair with the rope from the curtain blinds wrapped around his neck about to jump. Thank God they were on the ball, managing to stop him from doing anything to endanger himself. So where did he get this idea, he does not have access to newspapers at home or school and would not normally be encouraged to watch the news. Did he therefore just catch a fleeting glance of the execution on television and does this not show how quickly he can pick things up proving that our son is more intelligent than he may be given credit for. I need not tell you the curtain blinds disappeared that same afternoon and have not been replaced. In fairness to Hope Lodge neither my wife or I blame them for this incident, it was Christopher's speed and agility that would have taken anyone by surprise. What I applaud is the immediate action they took to prevent anything similar happening in the future.

As parents we have noticed an incredible difference in Christopher, in his behaviour patterns, he is certainly tearing far less of his clothes, in his speech because the clarity of his words has improved beyond all recognition and with his diet as he is eating a far bigger variety of foods.

Sure most of them are still very textured but we never thought we would see our son eat things like fish and beef burgers.

It is true to say that since Christmas, when incidentally he took part in the school nativity, he has made so much progress. Yes, he does still have those days when he gives his teacher hell but then that is the nature of the beast. Any child with autism is likely to blow a fuse for the least little thing, the difference now though is how that behaviour is dealt with using a positive response and avoiding anything that might add fuel to the fire. As you have read earlier Chris had an abscess on a tooth and during this period his only way to tell anyone it was hurting was to become violent, attacking his peers, teachers and us at home but through a unity between teachers and us, his parents, we have kept control.

It is this unity, a bond or perhaps better words would be understanding and trust between the classroom and home that has helped us to understand our little autistic lad who just under a year ago was almost lost to us all. Now, with the help of expert teaching staff Christopher is finding his way in life, we as parents recognize the progress he has made and understand the many cogs and wheels that make up this complicated disorder.

Before telling you of some fantastic news let me just mention another area where Christopher has improved beyond measure, his toilet training. There are good days, there are bad, sometimes there are several accidents in one day but compared to how Chris was a year ago the improvement is amazing. He may not make the toilet in time but is now, both at home and at school telling us when he wants to go. So what if it's too late, he's moving in the right direction.

Two things have happened in just the last week that have truly amazed Tina and myself and I have to admit brought tears to our eyes. How does any parent feel when their child spells and reads their first word? We were so full of emotion when we picked Chris up from school last week to be told he has recognised his first word. "Tom." All weekend Christopher lamented "Te O Ma, Tom, Te O Ma, Tom." I actually wrote the word on the computer in large letters and he immediately responded "Te O Ma, Tom." Fantastic, our little chap had started on his reading career; I just wonder what word will be next.

You could have blown us over with a feather when Christopher's teacher said, "And there's more!" More, what could possibly be better than our son reading his first word? Chissy's teacher had kept it quiet but back at the start of May she had nominated him for an award for his progress. This was open to all children across the county.

She wrote, "Since joining Hope Lodge School in September two thousand and six, although Christopher continues to need two to one support, he has progressed from displaying severe challenging behaviours on a daily basis, stripping naked, ripping his clothes together with other inappropriate behaviours which prevented him from accessing any areas of the curriculum.

To being able to be in his classroom with other students, demonstrates greatly improved language skills and generally displaying more appropriate behaviours which has enabled him to now access all areas of the curriculum, school and the environment."

Hang on a minute; was this our son she had portrayed? It most certainly was and the real icing on the cake was the letter his teacher had received recently confirming that our little angel had indeed won the award in his age group, for the pupil that had made outstanding educational progress and significant personal development. I cannot start to tell you, as Christopher's parents how proud we are of him. Neither will we ever be able to thank the staff in his class who work tirelessly to make something like this possible.

I call Chris an angel, but believe me he is far from that when the mood takes him but never have I heard the staff raise their voices or respond in an angry manner, even when Chris has physically attacked them and they have been clearly hurt.

Just so you can, for want of better words, get it from the horses mouth I asked Christopher's teachers to pen their thoughts on his first year at the school. Two of them joined together to write the following.

When Christopher first started with us at Hope Lodge School in the autumn of two thousand and six he proved to be extremely challenging which limited his time spent in the classroom. It became necessary to provide a separate classroom for Christopher, which enabled him to access areas of the curriculum in a safe, quiet environment. Christopher's behaviours at this time involved targeting fellow students, ripping his and the staffs clothes, stripping naked, pinching, kicking and biting. These behaviours were often accompanied by extremely loud screaming and bizarre obsessions, which included putting mud or paper into his mouth to chew it up and then throw it all over the windows. The same behaviours then transferred to the Lodge, the classroom and home.

Staff constantly tried to find positive reinforces to break the behaviour. Finally we hit on the idea of a whiteboard. It was fixed to the wall in his small room and Chris was encouraged to use this as a throwing board and at the same time he was prevented from throwing thing at the windows. This led to lots of fun or "Gloop" play. Gradually this was phased out and replaced by drawing and writing on the whiteboard, which in turn led to drawing on white sticky labels. From there he was encouraged to use all sorts of stickers and to encourage waiting a sand timer was introduced. This proved to be such a positive enforcer and incentive to keep him on task.

During that difficult time it became necessary to request additional funding so that Chris had two to one support. Fortunately this was agreed and it enabled a high level of consistent care, one member of staff working with Christopher whilst the other prepared the next task. The positive reinforcement of stickers has enabled Chris to gradually integrate back into the classroom where he can now access all areas of the curriculum in a small group setting. Working in these small group sessions has enabled Christopher to move on even further and he engaged in the whole school Christmas concert and regularly attends the twice-weekly whole school assembly.

Much of this improvement can be put down to the introduction of two to one care.

Another of Christopher's teachers told of two memorable moments that she recalls.

"I remember when Chris could not sit still for more than a minute, he threw food, plates, cutlery and water across the room. He used to chew food and then throw it on to the ceiling, the walls and the windows. He kept crawling under the tables, standing on the chairs and was forever trying to get away. The best day I remember was recently when Christopher stayed at the table all through lunch and asked very nicely for ryvita and honey."

The fourth teacher in Christopher's class, yes four teachers for three children, said that she most enjoyed it when she encouraged him to use the computer for the first time. He was watching his classmates and taking a real interest, it was so lovely to see so I decided to ask him if he would like to try. Surprisingly he sat down and played on the games and actually completed the "Matching" task.

Having read this chapter I am confident that you will have recognised the brilliance and professional approach adopted at Hope Lodge School. I know there are other schools out there that specialise in looking after children with autism but in my opinion there are clearly not enough. It is my wish that this necessity be recognised by World Leaders and that they take it on themselves to do more for the ever-growing number of autistic children.

Chapter 28
Home From Home

Certainly one of the most difficult decisions that Tina and I have ever had to make was whether we send Christopher to a residential school. The agony and the heartache that we have both gone through is almost impossible to put into words. Our son was only seven when we had to make this decision, still our little boy, the baby of the family, was it fair to send him away from his mum and dad for four days a week. Let me tell you that still to this day I am not truly happy in my heart about our little boy being away from us. Not being able to see him to his room or tuck him into bed is a hard pill to swallow but worse than that was on his eighth birthday when he wasn't in his bedroom at home when we got up so we could sing Happy Birthday to him and give him a lovely cuddle.

When we made that difficult decision we had to cast our feelings aside and decide what was probably best for Christopher and to give him the best possible chance to make as much progress as he could as soon as possible. Basically Christopher's learning extends beyond the hours he spends at school because he is being looked after by experts in the field of autism for twenty-four hours a day. I am not saying we never spend time with Christopher in the evenings when he is at home, of course we do, but we do have to spend time with our other son as well. You might think well why doesn't one parent look after Christopher whilst the other looks after Charlie but it just does not work like that. For the great majority of the time Christopher needs that two to one influence and care and so Charlie tends to lose out.

To soften the blow every Wednesday evening the three of us, that's Tina, little Charlie and myself religiously visit Christopher at the Lodge and spend a couple of hours playing with him, either in the art room or now the weather is better in the playground. We have only seen his bedroom once, when he first moved in, for we are not permitted into that area to protect the other resident's privacy but as I have already said it is so difficult to see someone else take him off upstairs when we leave. Before I cheer you all up and tell you how magnificent the Lodge and the staff are let me just tell you about one other niggle that we have. As the law now stands any residential school is governed by the same rules as a care home. When we attend meetings and social services refer to Christopher as being in care it makes my blood boil and every time I make sure they fully understand that our son is not in care and that we as parents have full control over him. The one thing that would see Tina and myself decide to have Christopher home each evening is if we feel that social services are interfering too much or trying a take over bid for our child. That decision would never be influenced by the way he is looked after within the Lodge, the staff are brilliant with Christopher but we will not tolerate anyone telling us how to bring up our children. We are being reminded more and more often that one day Christopher will be in full care, maybe, who knows what tomorrow may bring but until that day there are only two people responsible for our son's destiny.

Now that I have probably made many of you very sad I had better find a way of cheering you up. What better than to tell you about the positive side of this wonderful establishment. Over the months that Chris has been at the Lodge it has almost become an extension of our family home.

All of the staff are very friendly and so understanding of our feelings, none of them ever demonstrating the slightest attempt to usurp our parental duties when we are around. They are always so caring and loving towards Christopher whether he happens to be in a good mood or if he is throwing a tantrum. If patience is a virtue then the Lodge is crammed pack full of very virtuous people, dedicated to the children they look after. On almost all of our visits we see at least one of the children giving someone a hard time but never have we heard any member of staff raise their voice or treat the child in any thing but a loving way.

The Lodge is set in a fairly old building with about fifteen bedrooms upstairs, split more or less evenly between boys and girls whilst downstairs there are two lounges, an art room, a soft room, a very spacious dining room and a sensory room which staff would like to improve when funds are available. Who knows, by buying this book you will have donated a proportion of the cost to the charity and that may well be used in the sensory room. The children have a lovely playground, completely fenced in and about thirty meters by twenty meters in size. This playground is Christopher's favourite haunt riding his tricycle around like mad and not particularly caring who or what is in his way.

It was in the art room where a member of staff discovered Christopher's love for stickers, just peeling them off and sticking them on to a piece of card. It didn't take long before his sticker routine became an obsession, at the Lodge, at school and at home, we were all using hundreds of "stickys" as Chris calls them every week. That is until Christopher was introduced to a timer, just like a sand filled egg timer only somewhat bigger and somewhat more robust. Mind, one Saturday whilst at home when I was cleaning the car and had Chris sat in it in his harness, whilst Tina tried to clean up inside the house, he decided to throw his timer over his shoulder when he heard a van coming down the road. With the tailgate open you can probably guess what happened, yes daddy had to buy a new one. For sure though the use of the timer has slowed down the use of the stickers and more importantly taught Christopher to be prepared to wait.

The routine Christopher follows at the Lodge is pretty much the same every day, which suits an autistic child of course. He is awake somewhere between six and seven, has a bath at about seven fifteen and then it's off to the dining room for breakfast and his medication. Then it's back upstairs to clean his teeth and with this out of the way he is allowed to go to the playground and await the minibus, which will take him to school. With school over the minibus takes him back to the Lodge where it is straight upstairs to get changed after which Chris follows a photo schedule, generally spending time in the soft room or the playground before tea at around five fifteen. It's away to play again then until suppertime, which is around seven fifteen, followed by another bath and then he is generally tucked up in bed by about eight thirty.

Together with staff at school and us at home the staff at the Lodge continue to work hard on Christopher's diet, continually tempting him to try new foods, some with different textures, the highlight being a few weeks ago when they actually succeeded in getting Chris to put a pea in his mouth. It didn't stay there long but maybe next time.

Whilst at the Lodge Chris has still managed to find time for his Picasso impressions from time to time, he does not restrict these to his bedroom at home but the Lodge has one big advantage over home in that they have staff on patrol throughout the night and are therefore more likely to spot him at work and confiscate his materials

From the very first day that Chris stepped into the building everyone has loved him, falling mostly for his cheeky smile and his happy go lucky singing episodes. I told you about Christopher's memory and having been there only a few days he was able to run out of his room and recite most of the names of staff members and they thought that was incredible.

Rather than just hang around the Lodge every evening the staff try to take the children out for little trips, sometimes to places like McDonalds other times perhaps to a park or beach. For Christopher this has proved to be a real challenge, not so much going out in the minibus but actually getting out at the destination. Being terrified of dogs I think he believes there is one around every corner but slowly and surely the staff are working with Chris to alleviate this problem. During the course of his time at the Lodge he has steadily improved and I am sure it will not be too long before he is willing to take part in many more adventures.

Chapter 29
Right Or Wrong

So, with our true life story nearly at an end Tina and myself have to ask ourselves one very serious question, "Have we as Christopher's parents done the right things for him, made the correct decisions, done enough to fight his corner ensuring his life will be better for our efforts?" I wonder what all of you the readers think.

We are not perfect parents, in fact I don't think they exist but we are the first to admit that maybe given the last seven years to live over again some things would have been approached differently. Some of our decisions have been governed by our financial situation but the really important ones, the ones that have had most impact on our children they have been made from our hearts.

There is certainly one decision we shall never regret, despite all of the hard work, the campaigning, the arguments and the heartache we went through to achieve our goal to find the best possible education available for our little boy, we know we were right to choose Hope Lodge. It is the uniqueness of this very special school that puts it at the top of the pile in our eyes. The ability for staff to almost read your child's mind so that they can keep one step ahead and the caring way those same staff members treat your child one hundred per cent of the time. When one looks at the "Queen's Gong" list in January and June where are these people's names? Some may say they're just doing their job but please trust me when I say these men and women do not see it as a job, they are truly dedicated people whose purpose in life is to improve the lives of others.

As I write I can tell you the school is due for an inspection by the OFSTED team and my only hope is that these inspectors do not draw their conclusions based on standards set for ordinary schools, they need to recognize the very special talents and teaching methods that Hope Lodge has maintained over so many years.

It is not just the teaching staff that impress, it is a true team effort at Hope Lodge, every person having his or her designated station but always willing to help someone they can see is having trouble. From the head teacher, to the office staff and the catering team there is nothing but respect for parents, they seem to understand how you feel and treat you accordingly. Such is the importance put on the parent teacher relationship that the school has a dedicated officer to help you with any problems or queries a parent may have.

As I have said maybe over the years we could have done things that little bit better, perhaps we may have changed some things but without doubt and I say this with a resounding "YES," we were without any doubt right with our choice of school for Chris, the results and his improvement over his first year evidence enough for anyone.

Chapter 30
What Lies Ahead?

Oh, if only I could see into the future, if only I knew how to use a crystal ball but alas like everyone I must wait until tomorrow to find out what comes next. I truly believe, that whilst we cannot possibly forecast our tomorrows we can do something now that may just have a bearing on our future.

Everyone of us can to a certain extent control our own destiny, if you like it is in our hands but for parents with autistic children we must not just think of ourselves we must take responsibility for our children's future, for they, unlike normal children will never, I fear, be able to do this for themselves. It is so important we plan for them now and fight to get better care for the adults with autism, for our children will be adults one day and if we have not done the necessary ground work to see they are looked after well it may be too late, we shall not be around for ever.

I am convinced that charitable organisations such as the Hampshire Autistic Society and the National Autistic Society are here to stay. They are so valuable to a nation that has an ever-increasing amount of children being diagnosed with a problem somewhere along the autistic spectrum. It is up to us as a nation to make sure that organisations like the two I have mentioned are adequately funded, to allow them to carry on their fantastic work. Perhaps for a parent with a normal child it is difficult to understand why these societies are so important but just ask a parent struggling to bring up a child with severe autism how they would cope without someone to turn to, where I ask, would Tina and myself be without the Hampshire Autistic Society or the school it provides, Hope Lodge.

On a personal note I look to the future with great optimism for both Christopher and Charlie. Charlie has his heart set on becoming a vet, as I believe I mentioned and although he is only ten Tina and I want to give him every opportunity to achieve his dream. If all goes well and we can afford the fees we want him to enrol in a school just about three hundred yards up the road from Hope Lodge, yet again another fantastic school with a fabulous record of achievement. Never without hope but knowing realistically that Chris will find it very difficult to accomplish GCSE examinations we want more than ever to see Charlie succeed.

Whilst Chris may not reach the academic heights of his brother I am full of confidence that he will continue to improve in the years ahead, providing the funding for him to stay at Hope Lodge remains in place. I am sure he will present many challenges throughout his life but whilst Tina and myself are able we will continue to help him deal with his problems.

As for my wife and I we shall continue to work hard, enabling us to do more for our family. Of course we want to turn at least one of our dreams into reality, by having enough money to buy our motor home which will give us the chance to take regular little breaks with both Charlie and Chris and thus become independent once more, never again having to ask for help in the form of respite and never again giving anyone the opportunity to say we are selfish.

Chapter 31
The Wow Factor

Without any doubt the most important reason for me writing this book has been the desire to raise awareness of autism and the struggle for those people whose lives have been affected.

To achieve this successfully I will have had to appeal to your WOW factor. What do I mean? Somewhere between the front and back cover I will have had to have written at least one thing that has made you take a step back and think to yourself, "WOW I did not know that," or "WOW I did not realise how autism could change a families life."

I want this message to reach persons from all walks of life. The politicians and professionals, who are supposed to look after us, medical and social professionals, that they may pick up on something that up to now has not stirred their Wow factor.

Normal, everyday working class people so that they are able to understand better when confronted with autism and last but not least the many millions of people throughout the world that find themselves deep within the clutches of the autistic spectrum, that they may find strength, perhaps advice and the confidence to fight on.

Remember I told you I had to give up my driving school and then helped Tina with her business, which happens to be based on Network Marketing. I am appealing to each and everyone that has read this far to do some networking. Please spend just a little time each day for the rest of your lives making someone you meet aware of autism, perhaps aware of this book and aware of the struggles that so many face on a regular basis.

As I said at the very beginning life is all about choices. You can choose to lie down, give up, filled with despair or like my wife and I choose to fight for what we believe are our children's rights. We will spend the rest of our days fighting, not just for our children but also for everyone trapped within the syndrome.

I have especially written a poem for autism and have decided to include it as a finale` to my work. Like the book I pray that my words may touch some of you and give strength to those who need it. Incidentally if you would like a framed and signed copy of this poem please visit our website www.smartgiftsfromhome.co.uk. A proportion from the sale of the book and poem will be made to the Hampshire Autistic Society.

From now on please live your lives with your eyes wide open, not closing them as an act of convenience because you think you are not directly affected. Everyone needs to play their part to ensure that the best available care is in place, that never again will people have to fight for what should be rightfully theirs.

Autism may not directly affect you right now but life can be cruel and none of us knows what is around the next corner.

A Poem For Autism

Our son is autistic, so what the hell
You look at him most times you never could tell
There may be a tantrum, some screams at his Bruv
But then there's the cuddle that shows us his love

Why should we worry, we can't change him now
We must press on forward the question is how
I'll tell you the secret; we'll hold our heads high
For we're stuck with this problem till the day that we die

We'll let no one torment us, give us a hard time
Very few understand, far less give a dime
We'll make sure we tell them, yes announce full of pride
Our son is Autistic we have nothing to hide

We call on all parents with kids just like Chris
To help raise awareness of problems like his
They all deserve more so don't miss a chance
Shout loud; shout often their lives to enhance.

Written by Charles Parker and dedicated to his son Christopher
and autistic children everywhere.

Printed in the United Kingdom
by Lightning Source UK Ltd.
123158UK00001B/316-369/A